One Hundred
Glimpses
of
Our Lady

One Hundred Glimpses of Our Lady

Maurice Nassan

Sheed & Ward

London

ISBN 0–7220–6346–6

Published in Great Britain in 1994 by
Sheed & Ward Limited
14 Coopers Row
London EC3N 2BH

Book production Bill Ireson

Photoset by Waveney Typesetters, Norwich
Printed and bound by BPC Wheatons Ltd, Exeter

Introduction

Devotion to Our Lady must be based on sound theology, which means it must grow out of Scripture and tradition. She must always be seen in her relation to Christ. She is wholly and completely related to him. This means seeing her in relationship to great biblical themes, the Old Testament prophecies and types, the revelation of the Holy Spirit in the New Testament, the Word of God made flesh, the kingdom of God, the redemption and the resurrection. Mary has her part to play in all these and our prayers should be directed to her in them.

Some Christians have regarded devotion to her as peripheral. She happens to be there in Scripture but only in a minor role. We do not, of course, think of her in that way. We see her at the very centre of Christian devotion with her Son giving warmth and comfort and strength. The Second Vatican Council saw 'Mary, the sign of created hope and solace to the wandering people of God.' Christianity is the people of God on pilgrimage; a human caravan making its way through the dust and toil of the world to a promised land. By her act of obedience to God's will she gave this hope through the birth of her Son. Thus she opened the way of grace for all by giving them the source of all grace.

There are different themes treated in this book. Mary, like a diamond shines forth from different angles and points of view. We can pray to her as immaculate, as a virgin, as mother, as queen, as in sorrow or in joy. They are all subjects for meditation and for the increase of our love and devotion.

The Dowry

During the reign of James I, who died in 1625, a paper, now in the British Museum, was discovered giving an account of a picture described as very ancient, and known to have been in the church of St Thomas's hospice in Rome. It portrayed a king and queen kneeling and presenting the island of Britain to Mary saying 'This is thy dowry, O loving Virgin, wherefore rule it.' The king in the picture is said to be Richard II, who died in 1399.

This is the proud title that Britain once bore. In few countries of the world were there more numerous shrines and sanctuaries raised to honour Mary. Her figure, carved in all kinds of material, was to be seen everywhere. It met people by the side of the road. It adorned churches and cathedrals. Each one had its Lady chapel with its statue. It graced the crown of England. The soldier wore it on his surcoat and the shopman painted it on his sign-board. People loved to link Mary's name with what was most beautiful. Many flowers were called after her such as marigold, maidenhair and Our Lady's mantle. Many streets and districts bore her name. A few survive in London: Marylebone, Ave Maria Lane and others. Very often she was represented in inn-signs. Thus the Angel is that of the Annunciation and the Star was Our Lady, Star of the sea. Huge crowds of pilgrims would flock to her shrines and sanctuaries. Kings, statesmen and famous soldiers would travel to them to obtain help in their hour of need. Prayer to Our Lady was part and parcel of their lives. It was as natural to them as the air they breathed. So much of this has been lost in modern Britain. And there has been nothing to replace it. Thankfully there are those who do their best to retain it. Britain needs the help of Mary and it is for that help we must direct our prayers.

Flowers

Our Lady in the past has been called by the name of flowers or plants. They are often mentioned in connection with her feast days. In an ancient primer she is hailed as the Rose without thorns, the Lily of chastity, the deep Violet of the valley of humility. In the early part of the eighth century the Irish invoked her in their ancient litany as the Enclosed garden, Branch of the Root of Jesse, Crimson rose of the land of Jacob. In England in the past the snowdrop was called the Purification flower. The marigold belonged to nearly all the feasts of Our Lady and the name seems to allude to the rays of glory round her head. An ancient poem speaks of it:

I was the favourite of the poor
And bloomed by every cottage door,
Speaking of Heaven's Fair Queen to men,
They love me for the name I bore.
There is no love for Mary now.
And faith died out when love grew cold,
Men seldom raise their hearts to Heaven,
Through looking at the Marygold.

Our Lady's smock became Ladysmock. Shakespeare alludes to it in his Spring song:

When daisies pied and violet blue,
And lady-smocks of silver hue.

The common maiden-hair fern was previously called Our Lady's hair. There are many other flowers connected with Our Lady's name because men loved to link her name with what is beautiful.

Mary's Month

April is the month of Spring and May, the month of growth. With April comes the passing of Winter, the green shoots and the joy of new life, but with May comes maturity of blossom and plant and life. The Jesuit poet Gerard Manley Hopkins wrote:

> May is Mary's month and I
> Muse at that and wonder why.

And later he answers his own questioning:

> All things rising, all things sizing
> Mary sees, sympathising
> With that world of good,
> Nature's motherhood.

May has always been a joyful month both in nature and among people. In mediaeval England May Day was a public holiday. All classes of the people were up with the dawn and went 'a-maying'. Branches of the trees and flowers were borne back in triumph to the towns and villages, the centre of the procession being occupied by the maypole, glorious with ribbons and wreaths. The month has been dedicated to Our Lady since people felt that all this joy is joined with her joy of motherhood. This ecstasy all through mothering earth which is felt in May magnifies the Lord since it is a reflection of his greatness, wisdom, goodness and beauty.

But all the glory that nature gives to its maker cannot compare with the glory reflected in her, the mirror of justice. She magnifies the Lord above all created things. She gave birth to the Lord of nature. She shared the joy of his delight in the pageant of beauty which nature presented to his eyes when he was a child. To her, as to him, nature was a symbol, a pointer to that divine uncreated beauty and majesty which was its source and origin.

The Will of King Henry the Seventh

My most merciful redeemer, maker and saviour, I trust by the special grace and mercy of thy most Blessed Mother ever virgin, our Lady Saint Mary; in whom, after thee in this mortal life, has ever been my most singular trust and confidence, to whom in all my necessities I have made my continual refuge, and by whom I have hitherto in all mine adversities, ever had my special comfort and relief, would now in my most extreme need, of her infinite pity take my soul into her hands, and present it to her most dear Son. And so sweetest Lady of Mercy, true mother and virgin, well of pity and surest refuge of all in need, most humbly, most entirely and most heartedly I beseech you.

(Modernised version of the sixteenth-century original)

Birds

Kings Henry the Fourth gave to the royal chapel of Windsor a statue of Our Lady of silver gilt; on her right arm she bore her divine Son who is playing with a bird. It has been suggested that the bird represents the soul of man. The emblem of Saint-Cyr represents Our Lady in a boat and Our Lord 'Flying' a dove with a string fastened to its leg and the end of which he is holding. The painter Barocci painted our Blessed Lady holding her divine Son and St John the Baptist in her arms. St John is rescuing a bird from a cat which is at our Lady's feet. Perhaps the cat is a symbol of the devil. The seal of Plympton Priory represents Our Lady seated with her divine Son on her knee and holding on her hand a hawk belled and hooded. A hawk was the symbol of the highest nobility. The two little straps that hold the hawk on the wrist are called jesses. Perhaps the hawk is a playful allusion to Our Lady as 'the Virgin from the root of Jesse'. The great silver-gilt image of Our Lady of Lincoln bore in her hand a sceptre with one flower set with stones and pearls and one bird on the top of it.

Bells

In the final chapter of his book *The Fool has Said* Beverley Nichols wrote: 'As I sit down to write this final chapter on a dark and stormy evening the church bells are ringing for evensong. They are fine old bells, and if you were to clamber up the steep stairs to the belfry, taper in hand, you would see that the two earliest date from 1585 and are chiselled with the inscription "Come, come, and pray." For three hundred and fifty years, in fine weather and in foul, these bells have echoed through the valley, and there was a time when people heard them gladly because they knew that the bells were praising God who was indeed a very-present help in trouble.'

Bells were frequently heard in ancient Britain and they were usually given names. A great number of them were dedicated to Mary. Some of the ancient inscriptions have survived such as:

I am called the bell of Mary, the excellent maiden.
Hail Mary, when you pray this way.
I am called Mary, Come with peace, O King of Glory.

Right across Britain from Lindisfarne in the north to Canterbury in the south and from the great shrine of Our Lady at Walsingham in Norfolk to St David's in the west the bells would ring out when the light broke in the morning sky and again when darkness closed in at evening time to proclaim the greatness of

Mary to whom the angel said that she was well favoured. The bells were known as the Gabriel bells – they spoke of the love of the people for the Mother of God.

A Last Salutation

The martyrs who died in Reformation times had a great love for Our Lady. It showed itself in many different ways. The great saint and martyr Robert Southwell, after being tortured ten times, was brought to the scaffold of Tyburn to be hanged. Above him was the scaffold and rope, below him the cauldron and the dreadful instruments for tearing him in pieces while still alive. And he prayed softly, 'Blessed Mary ever a virgin and all you angels and saints assist me.' Edmund Campion on his way, too, to Tyburn, showed his love for her in a gesture as recorded in the following description: 'In the splash and mud of a rainy December morning, Campion was brought forth from his cell. There were two hurdles in waiting, each tied to the tails of two horses. On one Sherwin and Briant were laid and bound; Campion on the other. The procession took the route by Cheapside and Holborn. A little further and the hurdles were dragged under the arch of Newgate, which crossed the street where the prison stood. In a niche over the gate stood an image of the Blessed Virgin that was yet untouched by the axes and hammers of the Iconoclasts. Campion, as he passed beneath, with a great effort raised himself and saluted the Queen of Heaven, whom he hoped soon to see. Christian Issam, a priest, who saw the martyrs on their way, always declared that they had a smile on their faces and, as they drew near Tyburn, actually laughed. There was a cry raised among the people: "But they laugh; they do not care for death."' That little scene surely reveals so well the love and reverence of pre-Reformation England for the Mother of God.

Broken Statues

All over Britain in Reformation times statues of Our Lady were being torn down and smashed to pieces and those empty niches and broken stones became symbols of a great emptiness and the passing of a beauty more lovely than the sunlight or the stars. We can still see some relics of these statues in empty niches or headless figures in cathedrals and churches. England's most famous statue of Our Lady of Walsingham was publicly burnt at Chelsea and that burning was one of many. This too meant the end of the pilgrimages to Mary's shrines. They were robbed of their rich tokens:

> the shrine shall be pillaged, and the gold spent,
> The jewels gone for light ladies' ornament.
>
> T. S. ELIOT

The pious devotions which ceased at the same time were easily condemned as idolatrous. Our Lady found herself as an outcast in the very land which had been called her dowry.

Our duty then is one of reparation. We cannot repair those statues. We cannot fit the broken pieces together; they have long crumbled into dust, but we can do our best to repair an ancient wrong. We who are descendants of that ancient tradition have set up our statues which are symbols for us of our love and reverence for the mother of God. It is our task to show our reverence and devotion to her and spread it about us. There is clearly a great need for this in our modern age.

Inn Signs of Mary

When so few people could read and write it was essential to have some way of identifying shops and inns where travellers could be put up for the night. It was only at the beginning of the last century that the system of numbering shops and houses came into existence. Before that, taverns and shops were identified by house signs, that is, painted pictures hanging usually from a framework of iron. It was only natural in Catholic England that many of these signs had a religious significance. And, as one would expect, many were inspired by devotion to Mary.

There was a large number of inns with the Salutation sign. Originally this was a painting of the Annunciation. Later, when the Puritans ruled England, the subject was changed. The title Our Lady was sometimes used but much more frequently it was the Virgin. The Angel was a very common inn sign. At first it also was a representation of the Annunciation but at the Reformation Mary seems to have been omitted from the picture. Our Lady of Pity was the sign of a bookseller in Paternoster Row, London; Charles Dickens, in *Little Dorrit*, writes of Bleeding Heart Yard; the sign of an ale-house was the heart of Mary pierced with swords. Another favourite sign was Seven Stars. It represented the seven-starred crown which the Virgin Mary was usually shown wearing. All this shows how devotion to Mary was interwoven into the lives of the people of Catholic England.

To Our Lady

Dear Mother, in whose eyes I see
All that I would and cannot be,
Let thy pure light for ever shine,
Though dimly, through this life of mine.
Though what I dream and what I do,
In prayer's despite are always two,
Light me through maze of deeds undone,
O thou, whose deeds and dreams are one.
And though through mists of strife and tears
A world away my star appears,
Yet let death's sunrise shine on me
Still reaching arms and heart to thee.

E. NESBIT

Advent

Before any exciting event there is the joy of expectancy. It is this joy that Christians experience in Advent. They give voice to it in their prayers. It is true that this may not rise to a high emotional pitch, but there is no doubt that it is there in the Church's life. For Christians are awaiting for the curtain to rise on a magnificent drama in which the glory of the Lord will be revealed and the whole world stage flooded with transforming light. In that light they shall see light. For the feast of Christmas celebrates the coming of God into his creation transforming it by his presence and giving it a completely new dimension.

Mary had her special Advent. She knew the child was within her womb. Every mother knows the joy of expectation, the awaiting the birth of her child. During all the months and weeks before the birth of Christ, Mary's thoughts must have been turned inward to the one in her womb. One can imagine some of the questions she would have asked herself. What would the child be like? Would it be strong and healthy? She had, of course, some of the answers. They were given to her by the angels. She heard that her child was to inherit the throne of David and found a kingdom. Her knowledge of Scripture coupled with her virginity would have told her that he was the one her race had longed for. She knew that he was the holy one of God with a special mission on earth. Mary then must have experienced the joy of anticipation. Just as we during Advent look forward to the coming of Christ with his special gifts and blessings so did she, but in a far more intimate way since she was the one who was to give him to the world.

Women of Prophecy

The Bible is the book of salvation. Its history is salvation history. From Genesis to the Book of Revelation the theme of salvation is met with. St Augustine wrote: 'In the Old Testament the New Testament is concealed and in the New Testament the Old Testament is revealed.' For the Old Testament builds up to the coming of Christ, the central figure of Scripture. But Mary had her part to play in all this as mother of the Saviour and one would expect to find some indications of her in the old dispensation.

Where can we see her foreshadowed? Surely, right at the beginning. In the story of the fall God tells Satan, 'I will put enmity between you and the woman and between your seed and her seed; he shall bruise your head and you shall bruise his heel.' God is prophesying that mankind descended from Eve will eventually gain the victory over the powers of evil. We read later that this victory will be gained through the work of the Messiah who is the seed of the woman, of Mary, his mother. That mother will be a virgin. Matthew quotes the prophet Isaiah's words: 'Behold a virgin will conceive and bear a son, and his name will be called Emmanuel.' St Luke also sees Mary in terms of the Old Testament. The words of the angel at the Annunciation are taken from Messianic passages. He sees Mary as the daughter of Sion spoken of by the prophet Zepheniah: 'Sing loud, O daughter of Sion... the Lord is in your midst... do not fear a warrior who gives victory.' Thus Mary is foretold in history before her actual birth.

Virginity

Did Mary make a vow of virginity in her earliest years? Theologians and exegetes in the past have asserted that she did, and that her words to the angel, 'How can this be since I know not man?' are a proof of it. But, why if she had taken the vow, had she become betrothed to Joseph? It seems better to say that her words to the angel showed that she was a virgin and decided to remain so in the future. Hence her choice of virginity came after the Annunciation and not before.

Because of this, Mary became the first person to choose virginity out of love for Jesus Christ. She was the first of a vast number. In an ordinary Christian marriage, the love, both natural and spiritual, of two married people transcends their sexual union. Mary in her virginity manifests this higher love. She made of herself a complete commitment to Jesus.

Mary thus became the exemplar of all those who dedicate themselves by celibacy out of love for Christ. For that is what celibacy denotes, the complete giving of self to the service of Christ. Those who take a vow of celibacy are showing the supremacy of charity as a virtue. They are giving unselfishly for the sake of the spreading of Christ's kingdom in the world. Those who are unmarried for the sake of the kingdom do not have children, instead they do their best through their work and prayer to make themselves fruitful in ways where others are not free.

The Annunciation Story

In the National Gallery there is a painting by Fra Lippo Lippi, of the Annunciation. The angel Gabriel kneels before the seated figure of Mary. His hair is as bright as the Virgin's and he is glorious with gold and scarlet. He comes as to a royal audience. A great cloth of gold covers the Virgin's high-backed throne and continues as a carpet under her feet. Round her head is a golden radiance. Behind her the wall of the house has been cut away to reveal the internal arrangements. One can see a great bed richly ornamented and covered with a coverlet of gold brocade. This is only one of the very many pictures painted of the Annunciation. But what was the reality? What actually took place? St Luke paints a picture in words of the scene but even his picture is not necessarily historical in all its details. He is doing what the artists were doing, bringing out something of the great mystery and splendour of God's desire for Mary.

What St Luke was doing was seeing the Annunciation against the background of the Old Testament. To take one example. The angel says to Mary: 'The power of the Most High will overshadow you.' This is to represent Mary as the shrine of a great presence recalling what happened in Exodus:

The cloud covered the Tent of Assembly
And the glory of Yahweh filled the dwelling.
And Moses could not enter the Tent of Assembly
because of the cloud that overshadowed it
And the glory of Yahweh with which the dwelling was filled.

13

St Luke would have known that passage well and no doubt Luke saw in Mary this shrine of God's presence, the ark of God's covenant.

The Meeting Place

On a tiny plot of ground at the end of a village street an immense event took place; one that affected the lives of all mankind. Here it was that mankind returned to God after sin had created the great rift from him. That little room in the village cottage was the meeting place of God and man. There he made his tryst, his rendezvous with mankind. And all this through the agency of a woman.

How extraordinary is the manner of reconciliation. The angel makes a request of a woman who is a virgin and determined to remain one, that she should have a child who is to be the Holy One of God. In this way the plan, of which St Paul speaks, hidden for ages in God who created all things, was accomplished. She, like the Church, played her part in what may be called God's conspiracy to save the world.

We enter Mary's thoughts on that great occasion only by pondering St Luke's account with devotion. We can listen to the words spoken by the angel to Mary telling her that she was well-favoured with God. We can see her stupefaction when the angel announced his message and we can gather something of her humility and simplicity at her reply. It was on this occasion that the incarnation took place. St Luke shows us that it was the work of all three persons of the Blessed Trinity: 'The Holy Spirit will come upon you', he said, 'and the power of the Most High will overshadow you; therefore the child to be born will be called holy, the Son of God.' There is much to think about in this work of the Trinity whose purpose is to redirect the history of the world. In Mary's womb will be the one who in his human and divine nature will bring this about.

The Response

Mary's response to the message of the angel was queenly. In that moment she was confronted with something of unprecedented magnitude, something that would exact a trust in God reaching out into a darkness far beyond human comprehension. And she gave her answer simply, utterly unconscious of the greatness of her act.

ROMANO GUARDINI

Fear

Fear has many causes. Some great disaster can create it as, for example, a house catching fire. There is the fear of the unknown felt by a traveller journeying through dangerous country, and there is fear based on worry.

But there is a kind of fear which is very different. This is expressed by those in the Book of Revelation who cry out:

Who shall not fear and glorify thy name, O Lord?
For you alone are holy.

It was this kind of fear that Mary experienced. When the angel came to her and said, 'Hail full of grace, the Lord is with you' she was greatly troubled. But the angel said, 'Do not be afraid, Mary, for you have found favour with God.' Mary's fear was reverential. It arose because she realised that she was in the presence of greatness and holiness. She felt something of the majesty of God in the mystic experience she was undergoing. It was the kind of fear that Abraham felt when he cried out: 'I will speak to my God though I am but dust and ashes.' Peter felt it

15

when he knelt at the feet of Christ and said, 'Depart from me, Lord, because I am a sinful man.' He felt the vast gulf between his weakness and the greatness and holiness of Christ. Mary too felt a gulf between her weakness as a human being and the power manifested by this angel from God. The heavenly radiance about her overwhelmed her for a time; this light from Heaven puzzled her humility and filled her with wonder. But then, to quote some words of St John of the Cross, 'All her former fears fall away, and she knows clearly that she is free and sings with joy to see herself in such serene and tranquil peace.' Her fear gave way to joy, and she could later sing 'Magnificat'.

The Husband

Joseph's outstanding characteristic was his abiding faith and confidence in God's regard for him. This faith was his strength in all his troubles. And these were many. In fact every time he is mentioned in Scripture he is in trouble. Mary, we are told, was with child 'before they had come together' and he was naturally puzzled as to how this could be, knowing Mary as he did. He even thought of sending her away to protect her. But he never lost faith in God and he received his reward through the coming of the angel who gave him the answer that Mary had conceived through the power of the Holy Spirit.

Then there was more trouble. His task was to take the mother to Bethlehem and find a lodging where she could have her child and the only place he could find was a stable. Joseph has been called the shadow of the Father. We can think of him kneeling by Mary in the stable awaiting the birth of Christ. With what great wonder he must have waited. A shadow has a likeness to the reality. As guardian of the coming child he reflects in himself the office of the Father in Heaven. Though not the natural father, in love, duty and position as head of the family he had the office of Father on earth. Joseph was close to God. His life was to be lived in union with him in a unique way. The great St Teresa of Avila said, 'If you know not how to pray, take St Joseph for your master, and you will not go astray.'

Mary and Joseph

In the Gospel we are told that Mary 'was found with child of the Holy Spirit'. And because of this Joseph was resolved to send her away quietly. Did this mean that Joseph thought Mary had done wrong? Surely this could not be true since he must have known her character well. Why then did he think of putting her away privately? One interpretation has been put forward which has much to say for itself. Could it not be that Joseph already knew that Mary had conceived by the power of God and that he was so overwhelmed by the mystery that he felt himself in some way a man apart from it. Since Mary had this great privilege from God he perhaps felt that he had no longer any claim upon her. It was better then to preserve her good name that she should go away quietly.

The vision that Joseph had soon made it clear where his duty lay. Mary was to remain and his task was to be the father to her child. He was needed to protect and guide the child as well as act as husband to its mother. So Joseph was told to give the name Jesus to the child and in doing so was to become the foster father of the Saviour of the world. We do not think enough of Joseph's part in salvation history yet his part was of the greatest importance. Scripture does not say a great deal about Joseph's qualities. It does call him a 'just man' but for the rest it leaves us to infer them. Clearly since he was given such a tremendous task and privilege he must have been one who was greatly loved by God.

The Holy Spirit

The Holy Spirit is the breath of creation. At the beginning of time his warm breath was felt upon the earth. We are told in the book of Genesis that the Spirit of God moved over the darkness and primeval chaos to bring harmony and light and life. But it is not only in the physical world that he performs his creative work; he also works deep down in the recesses of the human soul. There too he brings harmony, light and life. He is the Spirit of strength and illumination of mind giving us a spiritual vision which sees God at work in our world. He gives us mastery over our weaknesses. But above all he is the Spirit of love, imparting that spiritual fire which is none other than the transforming love of God.

When the angel said to Mary at the Annunciation that the Spirit would come upon her he did not mean that she had not experienced his presence before. From the moment of her conception she was under his influence. He was the sanctifier who worked in her to keep her holy. At the Annunciation he was present to preserve her virginity, so that her son would come into the world, not by ordinary conception, but by divine power. And just as her son was under the power of the Spirit, so she would be also. The Spirit was the guiding force in Christ's life, directing him to his allotted task and what was true of Christ was true of Mary. She needed the help of the Spirit in her life. She gave herself over to his guidance and he gave her the strength at the end to stand beneath the cross and watch her son dying upon it.

Mystical Rose

There is a verse which goes like this:

A rose grew up in a garden fair,
Mystical, fairy-spun.
The waves of its clustering silvern furls
Sprent with a myriad crystal pearls
Yearned for the morning sun.

The light rose up in the Eastern sky,
Breaking in shafts of gold.
The heart of the snow-white rose so fair,
Caught in a torrent of gilded air,
Burned in its leafy fold.

Shadows crept over the darkling earth;
The crimsoned sun went down.
The rain, like a shower of blood-drops, spread
On the gentle rose-buds drooping head,
A glowing ruby crown.

The Mystical Rose at Nazareth grew;
Pure as a spotless gem.
Joy was the radiant golden shower
The Light of the World shed on the flower
And grief, love's diadem.

Two Pictures

St Aelred, a saint of the twelfth century wrote: 'Eve in Paradise held a long conversation with the serpent and told him all the lessons that God had taught her and Adam concerning the apple; and thus the fiend by her talk understood at once her weakness and found out the way to ruin her. Our Lady St Mary acted in quite a different way. She told the angel no tale, but asked him briefly that which she wanted to know.' The saint was using these examples when speaking to nuns about talkativeness. His final sentence shows this: 'Do you, my dear sisters, imitate Our Lady and not the cackling Eve.'

Two pictures are summoned up by St Aelred's words, the picture of Eve and the devil and of Mary and the angel. Eve is the mother of the human race according to Genesis. She was tempted by the most cunning of all animals. She was fascinated by the sight of its green scales shining in the sunlight twisted round the trunk of the tree of good and evil. It told of wonderful possibilities for her and her husband if she took from the tree the fruit and ate it. This she did and brought disaster upon herself and the human race.

But all was not lost. God prophesied a new start through a woman and her son. So an angel entered a little room in a small province of the Roman empire and spoke to Mary. There was no demand made, no tempting, just a request to which she gave her consent. And so because of this a second Eve brought light out of darkness, hope out of despair, a great future where all seemed to have been lost. She now makes reparation for the evil the 'mother of the human race' had brought upon it and in doing so becomes the new mother in a much more meaningful and splendid way, of all human beings.

Nazareth

What do we know about Mary's life at Nazareth? If we are to keep to the Scriptures account of it very little. But we can gather something of the kind of life she lived there from the words of Nathaniel: 'Can any good come out of Nazareth?'; and also from the fact that we know her husband Joseph was the village craftsman. Clearly it was a very simple life. There were none of the forms of entertainment that we know so well, no novels, no newspapers. All Our Lady had for entertainment was the beautiful countryside and the company of her friends and Jesus and Joseph.

Did anything extraordinary happen? After all her son was the Son of God. Would he not at least have been seen as an outstanding personality with great intellectual and leadership gifts? Again Scripture indicates that this was not so. When he returned to Nazareth later on and made claim in the synagogue that he was the fulfillment of prophecy they were amazed at his words and said, 'Is not this Joseph's son?' And they even tried to do away with him. No, Mary led a very ordinary life with her son and Joseph; the kind of life any mother in a village would have lived at that time. She did simple daily chores, washed up, made beds, said her prayers and went to the synagogue on Saturdays. This does not mean that in her private life she did not have a special joy in watching her son grow up. She knew he was someone very special in God's eyes and she must at times have pondered over the mystery that surrounded him.

Sinless

Mother, whose virgin bosom was uncrost
With the least shade of thought to sin allied;
Woman! above all women glorified,
Our tainted nature's solitary boast;
Purer than foam on central ocean tost;
Brighter than eastern skies at daybreak strewn
With fancied roses, than the unblemished moon
Before her wane begins on heavens blue coast,
The image falls to earth.

WILLIAM WORDSWORTH

A Simple Life

By modern standards Nazareth was a very slow place – no television, films, radio, newspapers, books or Cook's tours. Nor were there any artificial means of entertainment. Most of the villagers no doubt lived most of their lives there, dying not far from the place where they were born. For entertainment they had to be content with one another's company and the beauty of sky and surroundings.

In spite of all this they were, one feels sure, no less happy than modern man. They could well have been been happier and more contented. Robert Louis Stevenson wrote:

The world is full of a number of things,
I'm sure we should all be as happy as kings.

Maybe we should, provided we remember that happiness does not come from the possession of many things. It comes from the heart. In other words it comes from one's inner attitude to life. Millionaires can be more miserable than beggars. The three people who lived in the little house at the end of the village street at Nazareth were perfectly happy in each other's company. They were happy too in their work amid rather primitive surroundings. This does not mean that they did not have the ordinary vexations of life, its troubles and its difficulties. It means that they knew how to meet them with equanimity. Of course the happiness in that home came largely from the presence of Christ. He radiated happiness about him.

And here is a lesson for us all. Christ is a means of happiness in our homes and in our individual lives however simple and ordinary they may be. Love is the basis of happiness and our love united with that of Christ brings its own special joy and peace. We may have lots of possessions or only a few but whatever we do have must not replace our love for Christ.

Dependence

Mary the dawn
    but Christ the perfect day
Mary the gate
    but Christ the heavenly way
Mary the root
    but Christ the mystic vine.

Mary the grape
    but Christ the sacred wine
Mary the cornsheaf
    but Christ the living bread
Mary the rose tree
    but Christ the rose blood-red.

Mary the fount
>but Christ the cleansing flood
Mary the chalice
>but Christ the saving blood
Mary the temple
>but Christ the temple's Lord.

Mary the shrine
>but Christ its God adored
Mary the beacon
>but Christ the haven's rest
Mary the mirror
>but Christ the vision blest.

ANON

Our Mother

Scripture is quite clear about Mary's motherhood of Christ, but is it equally clear about Mary being the Mother of us all? St Paul tells us that when Christ rose from the tomb he did not rise with his physical body alone, he rose also with his mystical body. St Paul also tells us that we rose with Christ just as we died with him. And St Paul makes it quite clear what follows from this: 'As in one body there are many members, but all the members have not the same office, so we, being many, are one body in Christ and every one members one of another.' And because Mary is the mother of Christ, and we are members of Christ's body, she becomes our mother also.

It follows from this that she is the mother of the Church. This was pointed out in the Second Vatican Council which stressed two facts about her. They were her part in the mystery of Christ and her place in the Church. 'The Catholic Church, under the instruction of the Holy Spirit, honours her as its most loving mother with all the affection of a son's love for his mother.' One section of the Council's Constitution on the Church is headed: 'On the function of the Blessed Virgin in the work of salvation.' This emphasises the part she had in winning us over to the love of God. She was not the Saviour but she was intimately connected with the work of Christ, 'Today', said the angels to the shepherds, 'is born to you a saviour.' She was the mother. She gave us the one who brought us out of darkness into the light so that we could be both adopted sons of God and children of his mother.

The Legend of the Salve Regina

The legend is told by a Cistercian monk of the twelfth century about the great St Bernard of Clairvaux. Fr Thurston, S.J., in his book *Familiar Prayers and their Origin*, translated it thus:

During the harvest the following prodigy happened. One night, when the blessed man was taking his rest with the monks sleeping all around him, he heard in the church the voices of angels clearly and sweetly chanting the praises of God and his Blessed Mother. On hearing this he got up unperceived and stole towards the church in order that he might obtain a clearer view of what was taking place. Thereupon he beheld the holy Mother of God with an angel on each side of her, one of whom seemed to be holding a golden thurible and the other incense. Under the guidance of one of these the holy Virgin proceeded to the altar itself, and there he heard sung by angelic voices the antiphon 'Salve Regina' right through to the end. This he is said to have learned by heart and to have written it down afterwards, and also to have sent it to the Lord Pope Eugenius in order that by the command of apostolic authority it might be held in solemn observance to the honour of the Blessed and Glorious Virgin Mary, Mother of God. All of which was carried out, as many still bear witness.

Evening Prayer

Fr Thurston's book, *Familiar Prayers and their Origins*, contains a Dominican's account of the devotions on board the Venetian galleys proceeding to the Holy Land in 1480:

> The third time at which men praise God on board of a galley is at sunset, for then all assemble about the main-mast, which is the place of meeting on a galley, and there they meet and sing Salve Regina. After the Salve, the captain's chamberlain blows a call on his whistle, and straightway standing aloft on the poop, wishes everyone good night in his master's name and again, as in the morning, shows the picture of the Blessed Virgin, on seeing which all say Ave Maria thrice, as is wont to be done on shore later at the sound of the bell.

Mother of God

The two most astonishing things about Calvary are that the one who hangs crucified upon a cross is God and the woman standing under it is the mother of God. If these were not facts but only legends Christianity would not exist. Yet when one thinks about it one realises what horrifying facts they are and ones that require deep faith to accept. It means that God is attacked with blasphemies, curses, and blows; attacked by the very creatures he created out of love.

Did Mary know that her son was not only flesh and blood but also divine? It is very doubtful. For to accept it amid the dreadful darkness and agony is perhaps expecting too much. She certainly could not have known it by reason alone. It would have needed a revelation and it is not likely that it would have been revealed to her. She was to be the woman of faith until the death of her son. Full revelation would come when her son revealed himself in all his glory of the resurrection. What she did know was that her son was an outstanding personality and someone sent by God to perform a particular task and that she had had the wonderful privilege of giving him birth.

For us it is important to contemplate the figure on the cross as far more than a man. The great mystery of the cross is the mystery of God himself, of God acting through the agency of flesh and blood. We must see in Christ the supreme revelation of the immense love of God himself and we must see in the mother at the foot of the cross, not only the mother of a crucified Christ but also the mother of a Christ who is both God and man.

The Handmaid

When God created our world he did not, nor does he, leave it to its own resources. He continually creates it by keeping it in being by his word. This is also true of all the people in the world. He preserves their lives, sustains them in existence. Without him they would fall into nothingness. But there is one element in them that enables them to break away from his will.

He gave them the great gift of freedom so that they could give him a response of love. This does not mean that he is not with them along the road of life. He does not force them along but he is close by ready to extend a helping hand.

It has been written 'that every (human) experience is a kind of annunciation, an annunciation that God wishes us to receive something, do something or endure something'. The Christian's reply to God should always be 'yes'.

This was Our Lady's reply. Her mystic experience was so intense and almost overwhelming yet, once she knew what God required of her, she responded quite simply to his request. There was no crying out that it was too much, no protestation that she was too unworthy, no fainting fits. It was the simplicity of her reply that is so remarkable. She knew from her reading of Scripture how God demanded a response of service from his chosen people. She was one of them and so his will was her will. He was all that mattered. This was the kind of simplicity that one meets in true sanctity; the kind that a Christian mother may have in the face of some great tragedy, the death of a child, for example. Even disappointments become appointments with God. All through the scene of the Annunciation one gets the impression of simple submission to the will of God.

Hope

Christian devotion loves to see the figure of Mary against the background of Old Testament history. In some mysterious way of God's providence history received its direction and momentum from what was to happen at Nazareth. God chose a special race to be his people so that from it one day a girl would be born who would become the mother of the Messiah. Mary could think back at her own ancestry as she attended the synagogue on Saturdays and heard the Scriptures read and expounded. She would have heard that a root would spring forth from Jesse. She knew well the story of the pagan Ruth who became converted to Mary's own religion and who married Boaz and from whose marriage came Obed, the grandfather of King David. Mary did not need to go to a place like Somerset House to find her genealogy. It was set out for her in the book read every Saturday. No doubt some of it would only become intelligible to her after Gabriel's visit. She would before that never have dreamed, for example, that the words of Isaiah 'a virgin will conceive and bring forth a child' would be true of her. Nor would she have seen in herself the answer to the many texts about the coming Messiah – that she would be his mother.

We, who can look back at history, can now see that Mary was the hope of mankind. We know that she was asked to undertake the task of being the mother of the Messiah and that it was in her response to that request that our hope lay and was fulfilled. Right through the Old Testament there rang a note of hope in a great future. That hope was realised. Now our thoughts are fixed on the future and our hope is centred upon Mary and her child with their abundant gifts and graces.

Ephesus

The Council of Ephesus defined that Mary was the Mother of God. It decreed that 'if anyone should not confess that Emmanuel is truly God and that as a consequence the holy virgin is the Mother of God, for she brought forth in the flesh the Word of God made flesh, let him be cursed'. Because of what Mary is the whole history of the Jewish race and indeed the whole history of the human race is centred upon her because it was God's intent to take human flesh and become a member of the human race in order to redeem it. In a real sense then the whole of human history is concentrated on that moment. Hence if one asks what is the meaning of human history and why did God choose the Jewish race to be his chosen people, the answer is to produce a woman who would be the Mother of God, one from whom God could take human flesh. The incarnation did not come as a bolt from the blue. It did not happen in a flash. That was not God's way of doing it. It was in the 'Fullness of time' as the apostle tells us that God sent his Son born of a woman, born under the law, to redeem those who were born under the law. God working within the history of Israel had Mary in mind. Not only was there the preparation of Israel but there was also the preparation of Mary herself. She must be ready for her great office. So she conceived immaculate; no stain of sin was to mar the soul of God's mother. Her greatness of soul was to be the witness to the greatness of God's mighty work in her.

Immaculate

When the term Immaculate Conception is used people often think of it in a negative way, meaning that Our Lady was sinless from the time of her conceiving Jesus. But it has a very positive aspect. As well as being free from sin she was full of grace. This does not mean simply that she conceived without sin. Grace is the glory of God shining in a human soul. It is God's embrace of love. Hence Mary conceived in love. St John of the Cross has some beautiful things to say about this union. For example: 'The thread of love binds God and the soul so closely and so unites them that it transforms them and makes them one by love, so that, though in essence different, yet in glory and appearance the soul seems God and God the soul. Such is this marvellous union baffling all description.' Again: 'When the light of a star or of a candle is united to that of the sun, the light is not of the star or of a candle, but of the sun itself, which absorbs all other light in its own.'

There is a danger of sentimentality, of other worldliness, in speaking of grace unless one sees it in action in everyday affairs. Our Lady was not some ethereal being. Though she was in soul beautiful and glorious it did not show itself in the exterior. She did the washing-up, made beds, cooked and did the normal chores a mother does for her child. No doubt her fellow villagers liked her but they would not have seen anything extraordinary about her. We know her greatness because we know what she was and can see in some way into her soul. For them she was an ordinary mother and wife. She had no haloes or odours of sanctity. Within her restricted life she was, we know, the greatest woman in the world.

The Name

On the feast of the Annunciation on March 25th 1858 the local people felt that the Lady would appear again. Early in the morning, carrying her candle, Bernadette arrived at the grotto and found it 'aglow with light' and the Lady already awaiting her. Bernardette was confused and expressed regret that she should have kept her waiting. But the Lady made a sign with her head that there was no need for apologies. 'I told her how happy I was to see her again,' said Bernadette afterwards. Then she took out her rosary.

The Apparition moved from above the rose bush, came nearer the ground and stopped under the arch of the vault. Springing to her feet Bernadette went forward her candle in her hand. She remained standing and appeared to talk to the Apparition face to face. 'Madame,' she said, 'will you be so kind as to tell me who you are?' How could she persuade the priests to build a chapel and come to the grotto in procession unless they knew this? She repeated her request and the Lady bowed and smiled. 'I do not know why', Bernadette explained later, 'but I felt more confident and I begged her once more to do me the favour of telling me her name.'

At this third entreaty the Apparition, who had kept her hands joined, opened her arms, then lowered them. She then joined her hands again and brought them up to her breast and said, 'I am the Immaculate Conception.' The Apparition smiled again, spoke no more and disappeared smiling.

DON MASSIMO ASTRUA

Flight

Whenever Joseph is mentioned in Scripture he is in trouble. He was troubled when his betrothed Mary was with child; again when there was no room at the inn for the birth of the child; also at the loss in the temple and the flight into Egypt. His troubles were Mary's also. She had her share of them. But Joseph was a man of faith; he trusted in God's providence; and Mary shared this sentiment also.

It is difficult to imagine Mary and Joseph as refugees, but that is what they became. We know little about their journey into Egypt. It must have been difficult and it certainly caused them pain to leave their home. What were Mary's thoughts? Here there is plenty of room for meditation. Both she and Joseph knew there was something very wonderful about Jesus they had to protect against the cruelty of Herod. They knew that God intended their child for great things. It is best to concentrate one's thoughts on the significance of the journey rather than try and imagine its route and nature.

Why should Mary and Joseph be on the run when they have the Saviour of the world with them, even though at the time they could not have realised this? Couldn't God have settled the matter more easily? But God does not normally interfere with the ordinary course of human affairs. He lets them go their own way. What he wants is complete faith in him and that is what Mary and Joseph had.

Our life is a testing time. Our faith is constantly being put to the test just as theirs was. We are not going to be freed from the ordinary daily ills and troubles. At times the skies grow dark for us as it did for them. They saw, as we should see, what the wise men saw, the star of God's guidance.

The Temple

The temple at Jerusalem was the epitome of Jewish religion and culture. It dominated the city just as it dominated the lives of the people. Jewish tradition said: 'He that has not seen the temple of Herod has never known what beauty is.' In its centre was the Holy of Holies, God's special dwelling place. It was in this temple that Mary and her husband Joseph found Jesus after three days of searching. There is a certain piquancy about the scene. The child was to be a new temple 'not made with hands'. He was to become the substitute of the great building where the rites of the Old Dispensation were celebrated. He was the living expression of 'The Holy of Holies'.

The angel had said to Mary, 'The child to be born will be called Holy, the Son of God.' One day the magnificent building of shining marble and glittering gold would be utterly destroyed. The living Temple also would be crushed to death after the curtain dividing the 'Holy of Holies' had been torn down.

Mary at this time would not have understood all these implications. The doctors in the temple had admired her son's intelligence, but she had not realised the importance her son put upon being in the temple. 'Did you not know', he said, 'that I must be in my Father's house?' The Gospel tells us she did not understand what he was saying. Yet in spite of all the anxiety of her search for him she united her will with his. She knew that his action had been inspired by some higher call. How often do we hear Our Lady's words: 'Son, why have you treated us so?' echoed by people in trouble? All of us have to learn the lesson of doing God's will both in hard times and in bright times.

Why Have You Treated Us So?

Those words 'Why have you treated us so?' have been a fairly common cry of Christians. They have been asked after some great natural disaster or at the birth of a handicapped child. When Christ's mother asked the question his reply was that his service of his Father must come first in his life. This was to be true during the whole of his life even though it might cause pain to others. We do not know how God's providence works in our world. We are too near to events to see all the answers. What we do know is that God expects us to have faith in him. If, for example, a child is born handicapped it is no reason to blame God. We have to accept that the world goes along in its own way, a way that sometimes involves troubles and difficulties. It is then that our faith in God is put to the test. Mary did not blame Christ for what he did even though his action caused her pain. She accepted his reason for it and pondered over it. There would be many occasions in the future when her son did things she did not understand but always, one feels sure, she trusted that all would end well. One obvious example that must have hurt her was when her son returned to Nazareth and was not only rejected by those whom he had known in boyhood but was even threatened with death. She knew that God's ways are not our ways. We are not in a position to judge the reasons for certain and troublous events in our lives. With Mary we should pray, 'Thy will be done.'

Song of Praise

There is never a crack in the ivory tower
Or a hinge to groan in the house of gold
Or a leaf of the rose in the wind to wither
And she grows young as the world grows old.
A Woman clothed with the sun returning
To clothe the sun when the sun is cold.

G. K. CHESTERTON

The Wisdom of a Child

We should not think of Christ talking to the doctors in the temple as a kind of child prodigy; one with immense intellectual powers. His human mind was limited just as ours is. He was a child of his time. What he did clearly show was his wisdom, that gift of the Holy Spirit that had entered into his life. He had, of course, been helped by his mother. The early part of his upbringing had been in her hands. She had imparted some of her wisdom to him. Scripture says of wisdom:

She is a breath of the power of God,
pure emanation of the glory of the almighty;
hence nothing impure can find a way into her.
She is a reflection of the eternal light,
untarnished mirror of God's active power,
image of his goodness.

This is the wisdom that the young Christ possessed. Within him was the breath of the power of God and he was the image of his Father's goodness. This breath of the Spirit was manifested in

35

his answers to the questions of the doctors. They were no doubt amazed about the depth of his knowledge of Scripture. How proud of him his mother must have been. He had passed examination with full marks.

The Song of Bernadette

A well-known Jewish writer, an unbeliever, was present in Germany during the Nazi persecution of the Jews. He and his wife made their way southward from Germany through France to escape from the Nazis. The Gestapo were after them and capture meant the concentration camp and the gas chamber. Their hope was to cross the Spanish border and sail for the United States. But they were stopped by Spanish officials and sent back. They found a dwelling place in the little town of Lourdes for their first night. On that first night the fugitive writer stood in front of the famous shrine and made a prayer, a cry of help. 'I do not believe in you', he said, 'and I must be honest in saying so but my danger is great and in my extremity, on the chance that you might after all be real, I ask your help. See my wife and me across the barrier and when I get to the United States I will write the story of this place for all the world to read. I ask for your help.' Having finished his prayer he returned to his hotel. Never, he told his friend afterwards, had he known a calm so deep. Strange though it sounds, the Jew, whose name was Franz Werfel, and his wife got safely through the frontier within the week. The first thing he did once safe in the United States was to write 'The Song of Bernadette'. Before he died he told his friend that in his terror at his plight he had come to know God and thereafter had never lost the sense of his presence.

Vision

One night, while St Ignatius lay awake, he saw clearly the likeness of Our Lady with the Holy Child Jesus at the sight of which he received most abundant consolation for a considerable period of time. He felt so great a disgust with his past life, especially his sins of the flesh, that he thought all such images which had formerly occupied his mind were wiped out.

Mary's Portrait

'She was grave and dignified in all her actions. She spoke little and only when it was necessary to do so. She listened readily and could be addressed easily. She greeted everyone. She was of medium height, but some say she was slightly taller than that. She would speak to everyone fearlessly and clearly without laughter or agitation, and she was especially slow to anger. Her complexion was of the colour of ripe wheat, and her hair was auburn. Her eyes were bright and keen and her pupils were of olive green tint. Her eyebrows were arched and deep black. Her nose was long, her lips were red and full and overflowing with the sweetness of her words. Her face was not round but somewhat oval. Her hands were long and her fingers also.'

This is no true portrait of Our Lady. It is an imaginative description by Epiphanius, Bishop of Cyprus, who died about 404 AD. What did Mary look like? We do not know. There is a painting by a Dutch artist, Dierick Bouts, who lived in the fifteenth century, of St Luke painting a picture of Our Lady. There is a legend that St Luke was a painter. There is no proof of this but we do know from his Gospel that he was a splendid word painter. No other evangelist tells us so much about Our Lady in such beautiful language.

The oldest representation of Mary in the world is in the catacomb of St Priscilla in Rome. There is no attempt at a likeness. In fact it would not be easy to see that it was Mary if it were not for the child in her arms and the man standing behind her pointing to a star – evidently the prophet Isaiah who compared the coming of the Messiah to a rising star.

Our devotion to Mary has no need of photographic likeness of her. For us it is not what she looks like that counts, it is what she is in herself – the mother of God and men.

Simplicity

She is not puffed up, does not vaunt herself or proclaim with a loud voice that she is to become the Mother of God. She seeks not any glory but goes about her usual household duties, milking the cows, cooking the meals, washing pots and kettles, sweeping out the rooms and performing the work of maid-servant or housewife in lowly and despised tasks, as though she cared nothing for such great gifts and graces ... Oh how simple and pure a heart was hers. How marvellous a human being is here. What great things are hidden here under this lowly exterior.

MARTIN LUTHER

A Letter of St Thomas More

Thomas wrote the following letter to St John Fisher with Our Lady of Barking in mind.

'Most unwillingly did I come to court, as everyone knows, and the king himself sometimes tells me as a joke. And to this day I seem to sit as awkwardly there, as one who never rode before sits in the saddle. But our Prince, though I am far from being in his special favour, is so affable and kind to all, that everyone, let him be ever so diffident, may find some reason for imagining that he loves him, after the manner of the London matrons, who are persuaded that the image of our Blessed Lady near the tower smiles upon them, as they look closely at it while they pray before it. I am neither so fortunate in reality to perceive such favourable tokens, nor of so sanguine a temperament as even to flatter myself that I do so. Yet such are his Majesty's virtues and learning and such his daily increasing industry in both, that the more and more I see his Majesty make progress in good and truly royal accomplishments the less and less do I feel this court life to hang heavily upon me.

The Image of Mary

If one shuts one's eyes and tries to think of a portrait of Our Lady one of a great number may enter into the imagination. It may be a picture by some great artist, a Botticelli or a Raphael or the statues of Lourdes or Fatima, or simply some picture of her that one has on one's mantlepiece or in one's bedroom.

Her real likeness, of course, eludes us, yet each person and each Christian country does have pictures of her which they regard as their own. When Bernadette saw Our Lady at Lourdes

39

she was not seeing her as she was at Nazareth. Bernadette saw a beautiful lady and no doubt Mary appeared in a way she knew would appeal to the little girl. The mediaeval painters never attempted to depict historical details by painting a girl in Nazareth against a Palestinian background. Fra Angelico, for example, painted her as an Italian and set her against the scenery of his own land. Such painters seized upon the fact that Christianity exists in all ages. What happened two thousand years ago concerned mediaeval Italy just as it concerns modern Britain. Mary is the mother of us all. She belongs to every age, country and person and everybody can represent her in the way that it appeals to them most. So to the Chinese she becomes a Chinese lady, to the West she takes on a European look, to the dark races she becomes dusky. In the celebrated Book of Kells in Ireland there is an illumination of Our Lady with her son. She wears a purple garment interwoven with shamrock, a plant she certainly never saw in Palestine. The world has dressed her in every kind of fashion, Renaissance, Flemish, Parisian. To some she appeals as Our Lady of Lourdes, to others Our Lady of Good Counsel and so on. Always it is what she is rather than what she actually looked like that is important.

The Artist's Vision

In appearance Mary was a simple Jewish girl, looking no doubt very much the same as others in the Galilean village in which she lived. She is one whose image has been painted countless times. It is not the task of an artist simply to reproduce a photographic likeness of a person; a thing he could not do anyway in Mary's case. His task is to bring out the soul in the face. Andrea Del Sarto was known as the faultless painter. In Browning's poem about Raphael the poet has been looking at a picture by him and seeing what is wrong with its anatomical details. He could put those right, 'But all the play, the insight and the stretch' was beyond him.

Ah! but a man's reach should exceed his grasp,
Or what's a Heaven for?

No artist can depict Our Lady's inner excellence perfectly, but in striving to do so they have produced beautiful works of art. Their task was to depict her grandeur of soul, her richness of grace, her wealth of love. So she who lived at Nazareth becomes dressed in rich embroidery, becomes crowned with a thousand crowns and covered with jewels she never saw in life. Artists are honouring her greatness, her plenitude of grace, her Immaculate Conception, her simplicity, humility, her faith and love. They are striving with canvas and paint to show her spiritual beauty through a physical medium. What the artists do in paint we, who love Our Lady, strive to do in our thoughts and imaginations. We may not be able to do what Raphael and other great artists did in paint but we can through our prayers learn more and more of what they strove to depict.

The Icon

Our Lady has been represented in a multitude of ways; among them are icons. The Eastern Church did not want to have beautiful girl models for their paintings of Mary as some of the Renaissance artists did. They did not want to dress her in fashionable clothes. They painted their pictures in a style that we might think at first stiff and formal. Certainly there was no attempt at realism.

Once every Russian home had its icon with a little light burning in front of it. The icon that is the most famous, the most ancient and the most loved in Russia, or was at the time, is that of Our Lady of Vladimir. Its original still exists in Russia. Unfortunately it has not been seen in a church but in an art gallery.

What was the unknown monk who painted the picture striving to do? He was endeavouring to express the spiritual through a material medium, trying to show holiness and purity and heavenly beauty. He was producing a prayer in paint. He wanted us not to be just onlookers but to pray with it. The face of the mother is full of tenderness and the sadness of the world. Her eyes look to the time when the child whom she clasps so closely to herself will suffer for us. For in the icon is pictured the incarnation and redemption and the wonderful beauty of a mother's love, which made it all possible. Let us hope that this beautiful icon, so old and so loved, may play its part in reconciling the Eastern Churches with the West.

Visitation Joy

Rita F. Snoden has written: 'The count-down to the first Christmas we now see as history's longest, most deliberately planned operation. It began in God's heart.' With Mary's acceptance of God's request the count-down was over. She accepted it not only with simplicity, but with joy. She goes with haste to tell her cousin Elizabeth all about it. 'Rejoice, rejoice, my spirit in God my Saviour', she said and Elizabeth in her turn responded with joy as the child leapt in her womb.

Joy is at the heart of Christianity. The Gospels are tidings of great joy. The angels sang their song of joy when Christ was born. It is these tidings that Mary brings to her cousin for she brings within herself the one who would give joy to the world. And Elizabeth rejoices and says, 'Blessed are you among women and blessed is the fruit of your womb.' The world was never to be the same again. Out of its darkness a new light shone, for

Mary was the source of a new light shining on the earth. This light came to banish despair, doubt and disillusionment and rouse faith and optimism in a great future.

This meeting of Mary and Elizabeth was not just a friendly meeting between relations, it was a meeting governed by the Spirit of God. Mary had conceived by the Holy Spirit and now when Elizabeth meets her she is 'filled with the Holy Spirit'. So the Spirit sings a song of joy in their hearts; a joy because the Lord is coming into the world to save and transform it. Out of a long Winter there will come new life and vitality 'a joy no man can take from you.'

This joy of Mary and Elizabeth we can all share. We can meditate with wonder at God's providential ways and we can rejoice in the knowledge that what God did for Mary was for our sake.

Magnificat

St John Berchmans has said: 'Souls are like mirrors, greater or less according to their degree of perfection. A small soul gives a very poor image of God. A large soul gives a very true and magnificent image of him. Hence Our Lady said in her prayer, the "Magnificat", "My soul magnifies the Lord"!'

Mary said of herself that she is very small and unimportant; it is God who gave her such importance that all nations would call her blessed. An artist at one moment has at the end of his bristle brush a shapeless smudge of pigment; but no sooner has he applied it to the canvas and put his mind, his vision, his artistic skill into the paint that it becomes a thing of beauty and a joy for all to admire and appreciate. So God, the great artist, took the dust of the earth and fashioned it to receive a soul and graced and purified it and enshrined it with his immense love. So he made a human being so lovely that she became his mother, the mother of the God-man who redeemed our world. The tiny was in this way magnified to greatness, and Mary could say 'the humble he has lifted high'. Mary showed her humility by her words of acceptance of the great task asked of her, and as a result she was 'lifted high'.

For us Mary is not just an artistic work of God. She is a woman who cooperated with his will perfectly giving him love for love. And because of that, and because God has done great things for her, we know that she has a great power with him and so we turn to her in our needs.

Faith

If ever there was a human being who knew what love really signified it was Mary. She possessed it in her heart and mind. Love itself in all its depth, in all its beauty, in all its wonder, was in her and about her because her child was love itself. She cradled the divine love in her arms.

Yet Mary was not in Heaven. She had to submit to the rebuffs of life. She had her anxieties and troubles. But at the same time she was a woman of strong faith. She did not continually look in upon herself as we are often inclined to do. Her faith gave her the vision to see the providence of God at work in Gabriel's message, in the Bethlehem journey, in the flight to Egypt and in all the trials that would send a sword through her heart. She must have seen the world in terms of her son. She pondered everything about him in her heart as she watched him at play or at work in the carpenter's shop.

St Leo the Great said, 'Faith is the power of great souls and the light that beats in faithful hearts.' This light of faith shone in Mary however dark the going was. After all the Holy Spirit is the Spirit of Light and his light had entered into her right from the beginning. The Spirit is also a power and it was through his power that she conceived her son. It was this light and power that gave her strength when she saw her son dying on a cross. Here was darkness, terrible agony and deep mystery. The son whom she loved was covered with a cloak of blood and wounds yet her faith stood firm. She did not cry out at the injustice and horror of it all. She knew her son went willingly to his death so she joined her will with his in an act of complete faith in God.

The Mystery

How much did Our Lady know about her son during his life on earth? How far did she penetrate into the mystery of his personality? These questions can supply plenty of matter for meditation. Scripture says 'God so loved the world that he sent his son into it.' This son had a human heart which loved in a human way but his love was also divine. How far did Mary understand that inward secret experience of Christ's love? This was a love which was an amalgam of the human and divine. In Christ there was a secluded region, the meeting point of God and man, a Holy of Holies, where only the High Priest himself could penetrate.

Mary would certainly not have understood all this. She had, of course, a far deeper knowledge of him than anyone else, but the inmost mystery of his being must have been hidden from her. She had all a mother's love for his humanity, a humanity which acted both as a screen hiding the divinity and as an expression indicating it. The divine in him, like a fountain, overflowed into the human, becoming a supporting power, not in the sense that the two became identical but because they acted as a unity.

What Mary saw was the very human Christ; a Christ who had a very special mission from God. She must have known that he was the 'Hope of Israel'. She could see that his mind and heart were filled with the love of God but the complete mystery eluded her. She wondered at the mystery and her response to it was, as always, a response of faith.

The Crib

The poet Crashaw wrote:

That the great angel-building light should shrink
its blaze to shine in a poor shepherd's eye.
That the unmeasured God so low should sink
as prisoner in a few rags to lie;
That Glory's self should serve our griefs and fears
and free Eternity submit to years.

We can meditate like that about the child in the crib but what were Mary's thoughts as she looked at him? She must have known the prophecy (Matthew 2.6):

And you, O Bethlehem in the land of Judah,
are by no means least among the rulers of Judah;
for from you shall come a ruler
who will govern my people Israel.

She must have been puzzled about the way of this ruler's coming. Centuries before, the prophet Isaiah had said: 'The Glory of the Lord will be revealed.' She certainly knew that in some way here in the crib was that glory. She would have accepted too that in some mysterious way the providence of God was at work so that her child would grow up to perform mighty works. As always, deep faith was required of her and she responded to it in its fullness.

It must have been hard for her to have her child born in

46

poverty. We can meditate on the scene and see so much of it for our benefit. We know that the 'unmeasured God' lay in the crib, that there was one who was immortal on his way to a terrible death, that one who was timeless was having a birthday, that he who was eternal had powers of growth. Our wonder should extend to the mother. The thought of her motherhood should raise our minds to the God of love and how her motherhood does indeed show forth the greatness of his majesty.

Christmas Night

God abides in man. He has put on the swaddling bonds of poverty and surrounded himself with the bleak and drab walls of a cattle stall. The mother looks down on her child she has given to herself and to the wide world; given one who has come to reveal the mystery of existence, one who is Truth itself. She herself knows little of this. She is a village girl who has had a unique child, one over whom she will ponder, filled with wonder until the full revelation comes. We are all born with this little child; he has come to give us new life and a mother who is not only our mother but the mother of God.

So much takes place within the dimensions of a stable. The world is about to be transformed. The darkness of the night is the darkness over the whole world, a darkness of sin it is now about to be flooded with a bright dawn as the Light of the World is born. He is one who will illumine every man who comes into the world. Mary is the beacon who has given this light. Mary knew that her son was to be in some way a light to men. Her virginity was a sign of his future greatness and so she was the instrument of God's plan for mankind. What that plan was she did not know. She looks down at her child with a mother's love. Her love for him being also a love for God who had done great things for her. Because of what has happened all nations would call her blessed.

Wonder

Foremost amongst those who, wondering, had heard what the shepherds told, was she who most it concerned, who laid it up deepest in her heart, and brought to it treasured stores of memory. It was the mother of Jesus. These many months all connected with this child could never have been far away from her thoughts. And now that he was hers and yet not hers – belonged, yet did not seem to belong to her – he would be the more dear to her mother-heart for what made him so near, and yet parted him so far from her. And upon all his history seemed to lie such wondrous light, that she could only see the path behind, as far as she had trodden it; while upon that on which she was to move was such dazzling brightness, that she could scarce look upon the present, and dared not gaze towards the future.

ALFRED EDERSHEIM

No Room at the Inn

St Luke tells us that when Mary and Joseph applied for hospitality it was refused because there was no room. This is what happened to Christ during all his life. People so often rejected him, could find no room in their lives for him because they were full of themselves or did not want him. He had no room to live in. He said of himself that he had nowhere to lay his head. In the end his own people had no room for him in their country and they did away with him by crucifixion. How this rejection of him must have hurt his mother. The little family who sought hospitality in Bethlehem could not blame those who refused to give it to them. They only refused because the inn was already full. They could have had no inkling of the nature of that little family.

Today there are many who refuse to accept Christ. They are so full of their own activities that there is no room in their lives for him. Christ knocks at the door of their hearts. He wants to share a meal with them but they keep the door closed against him. Fortunately there are those who do invite him in. He promised that if they did welcome him he would come and abide with them. St Paul could say, 'I no longer live but Christ Jesus lives within me.' As we enter in imagination the cave of Bethlehem let us remember that Christ is there so that we can be born again and live a new life; that we can invite Christ to enter into our being so that we can say with St Paul 'For me to live is Christ.'

The Christ-Child

The Christ-Child lay on Mary's lap
His hair was like a light.
(O weary, weary were the world,
But here is all aright)
The Christ-Child lay on Mary's breast,
His hair was like a star.
(O stern and cunning are the Kings,
But here the true hearts are)
The Christ-Child lay on Mary's heart,
His hair was like a fire.
(O weary, weary were the world
But here the world's desire)
The Christ-Child stood on Mary's knee,
His hair was like a crown,
And all the flowers looked up at him
And all the stars looked down.

G. K. CHESTERTON

Bethlehem

Think what a treasure the world became possessed at the first Christmas. From the creation of the world never before had such an addition been made to its precious things, its marvels, its magnificence, as by the birth of this child. Not all the collective learning of philosophers and sages comes anything near to the deep store of knowledge and wisdom which earth now holds in that little babe. Not all the united power of conquerors, kings and emperors can be put in comparison with the mighty power centred in this apparently helpless child. Not all the wonderful works of God's hand, the sun and moon and stars exhibit a fragment of the wonders of beauty which are to be found in this small infant. Had God on a sudden created another sun with sevenfold the splendour of the present there would not have shone so bright a light through creation as in the sight of the angels broke forth when the precious infant came into this world.

CARDINAL WISEMAN

The Star

Christ's mother is called the Star of the Sea and the more so because even on her head she wears a crown of twelve stars. Jesus is the Light of the World, illuminating every man who comes into it, opening our eyes with the gift of faith, making souls luminous by his almighty grace; and Mary is the star, shining with the light of Jesus, fair as the moon, and special as the sun, the star of the heavens, which is good to look upon, the star of the sea, which is welcome to the tempest-tossed, at whose smile the evil spirit flies, the passions are hushed, and peace is poured upon the soul.

CARDINAL NEWMAN

A Child Speaks

Little Jesus, wast thou shy
Once, and just as small as I?
And what did it feel like to be
Out of Heaven, just like me?

Didst thou kneel at night to pray
And didst thou join thy hands this way?

And did thy mother at the night
Kiss thee and fold the clothes in right?
And didst thou feel quite good in bed,
Kissed and sweet, and thy prayers said?

FRANCIS THOMPSON

The World's Greatest Love Story

The Annunciation is the starting point of the world's greatest love story. It is greater than the story of creation. It was at the Annunciation that God who is love itself united himself to mankind and became like us in all but sin. 'The Word became flesh and dwelt amongst us.' To do this he chose a little village girl to be his mother; one more beautiful in soul than the rest of humanity.

A beautiful legend relates that the Greek god Apollo laid his lyre upon a stone and the dumb rock absorbed the last strains of the melody. Whoever would find the stone could, if he placed it to his ear, hear the slumbering song of the god. In every soul there is a note of the divine. God has given to it his own image. Every heart was made to sing the praises of God. The song of praise that rose from Mary's heart was so great that all ages would call her blessed.

It was when the fullness of time had come that the Holy Spirit came upon Mary and the power of God overshadowed her so that the God-man was conceived within her. It was for that moment that the whole of time was waiting. This was the high point in human history. Now all history would be diverted into new channels as those who had lived in darkness would see a new light, the Light of the World. The river of time which had had its source in the creative act of God had come to its term and henceforth would become 'a fountain of water springing up into eternal life.' Thus the God of love submitted himself to the restrictions of time so that we mortals might be united with him for ever.

Mother and Child

Mary has been honoured in a thousand different ways through the ages. Many beautiful things and places have been named after her. Great shrines and feasts have been devoted to her. And all this happened because of the fruit of her womb. Without that fruit Mary is nothing. All her greatness, her graces and privileges flow from it. That is why the mother and the child are inseparable.

Many people, it is sad to say, have torn Christ from his mother's arms, thinking they can worship the son and ignore the mother. They do not take to heart what Scripture says – that when the shepherd came they found the child with the mother, that when the wise scholars travelled across the world to find the king they too found him with his mother; that for long years at Nazareth he was with his mother; that when he lay upon the cross amid darkness and pain his mother was close by. The Church has always found the son with his mother.

And what does this mean for us? This association of God with man in motherhood and sonship shows us what human nature can become under the supernatural influence of God. In this picture of the child with his mother the human spirit finds rest. We cannot look upon the mother without our minds being raised to the love and power of God. We know that the child Mary holds in her arms contains all the treasures of wisdom and knowledge. She holds in her arms him whom the heavens and the earth cannot contain and in whose heart beats eternal love. Yet he before whom the angels bow in adoration looks to her for comfort and protection. How then is it possible for the mother to be thought of and honoured without reference to her son?

Beginning and New Beginning

In the first beginning the Spirit of God fashioned a world out of the dark womb of chaos; and what was a wasteland formed into a pattern of sea and land as the first dawn broadens across the landscape fertile and harmonious. Voices are heard where before there was universal silence, the cries of animals and the singing of birds in a garden of delights. Last of all man emerges, shaped into the image of his maker, with whom God walks on intimate terms in the cool of the evening air.

Into this idyllic scene chaos erupts in another form and human history is diverted from its high destiny by a serpent's wiles and human stupidity and pride. But all was not lost. The Spirit would once more move over a dead and chaotic world to restore its harmony and direct its destiny. And this he would do through the agency of a woman. 'The Holy Spirit will come upon you', said the angel to Mary. Mary at her Annunciation was made fruitful through the work of the Spirit so that her cousin could say, 'Blessed is the fruit of your womb.' It was the fruit of her womb that became the centre of a completely new beginning for the world. There would be new life and new beauty. The seeds that would not germinate in a godless world of sin would now blossom forth into resurrected life. So Nazareth became the fountain from which sprang the living water that would irrigate the world. It became the source of a living flame of love to warm a world that had grown cold. It became the centre of a mighty power whose impact would be felt by all mankind.

The Trinity

St Ignatius of Loyola in a meditation on the incarnation gives a picture of the three Divine Persons – Father, Son and Holy Spirit – looking down on a world of strife, sin and turmoil and deciding to send the Son into it to save it from itself. The picture is then focused upon a room in the village of Nazareth where Mary dwells. An angel is sent to her to explain how she who is a virgin can become a mother: 'The Holy Spirit will come upon you, the power of the Most High will overshadow you and the child to be born of you will be called holy, the Son of God.' So Mary became a mother through the power of the Spirit. Mary gave her free consent to what the angel asked but the Holy Spirit was at the very heart of her response. It was God who took the initiative not she. Her fiat was a masterpiece of divine grace and human liberty. Just as her Son was under the guidance of the Spirit all during his earthly life so it was with her. From the Annunciation until the foot of the cross he was her help and guide. The spiritual force which entered into her at Nazareth never left her.

Prayer at Walsingham

Erasmus, the friend of Thomas More, composed the following prayer while visiting the shrine of Our Lady of Walsingham.

May your son grant that in the imitation of your holiness, we may also be made capable by the grace of the Holy Spirit, of conceiving the Lord Jesus in the depths of our souls; and that once conceived we may never lose him.

Circumcision

On the eighth day after his birth Jesus was circumcised and given his name. Mary already knew the name because it had been given to her by the angel. 'You shall call his name Jesus,' the angel had said. She of course would have been present when her son was circumcised and she would have known the religious significance of the ritual, namely that her son belonged primarily to God. Every Jewish mother understood this. But for Mary the ceremony had a special significance. The name of her child meant that he had come from God to be the saviour of men and this occasion set the seal on his vocation. The boy was a member of the Jewish race but at the same time there was a mystery about him which she was to ponder over for many a day.

What Mary could not have known was what her son's name signified in terms of suffering and death. The blood flowed a little at the circumcision, she knew that; she did not know that one day all his blood would flow from him in crucifixion. Nor could she know, as she stood near him, that one day she would stand in darkness near her son transfixed with nails in hands and feet.

There is a great deal here for contemplation. That little eight-day-old child Jesus was to be our saviour and the saviour of all humanity including his own mother. Did Mary realise that here was the source of all her graces? Hardly so. She was to remain the woman of faith, to accept without knowing, to live in darkness in the presence of the light.

Beauty

To someone with spiritual insight the world has an inner beauty which is reflected in its outer form. The sunset is more than its chemical brilliance; flowers more lovely than their shape and colour; all nature more splendid than its changing pageantry. Such a person penetrates beyond superficialities to discover 'a beauty ever ancient, ever new' imparting a faint radiance of its own. To him the world shines with a divine luminosity.

But what part does Our Lady play for such a one? It is not her exterior that counts with him or her, but her beauty of character, her purity, her inner excellence. He sees the beauty of God himself shining within her. He understands also that amid material conditions she is there to raise mankind beyond sensual beauty to that supernatural beauty which will help to soften bitterness and hatred and create an inner sense of God's dwelling amid ugly and impoverished surroundings.

Our prayers open a door to her as our mother and helper. St Anselm prayed: 'Grant, I beseech thee, O God, that I may taste by love that which I taste by knowledge; that I may feel in the heart that which I touch with the mind.' That is how we should pray to Mary. Her beauty takes many forms. Deep down in all beauty is the mystery of the Spirit. From the beginning he was at work within her. His breath imparted to common clay an immortal beauty by fashioning it to a divine image. Since that is true of every person, how much more true is it of her who was made more like the divine than any other human being.

The Inner Life

It is clear that nothing can be known about the deep inner life of Mary in the sense that we have no record about her spiritual strivings, her aspirations and consolations and all that entered into her heart and mind. Mary must have valued this element of hiddenness and privacy. She speaks very little in the Gospels but we are told of her meditations. St Luke tells us that, after the shepherds had worshipped her child at Bethlehem, 'Mary kept in mind all these words pondering them in her heart.' And again, after the boy Jesus had been found in the temple, we are told in almost the same words, 'His mother kept all these things carefully in her heart.' It is clear also that though we may know little about what went on deep in her heart one can know something about it in general terms from what can be inferred from what she was in herself and from the circumstances of her life. Like any other loving mother she was 'wrapped up' in her child but her child was special and received a special love. She must too have pondered over the mystery of her child; who could he be who came from a virgin birth? She knew that God had done great things for her and the greatest of them was his gift of her son. Mary had immense things to ponder over but always her love for God predominated.

The Happy Morn

This is the month, and this the happy morn,
Wherein the Son of Heav'ns eternal king,
Of wedded maid and virgin mother born,
Our great redemption from above did bring;
For so the holy sages once did sing,
The he our deadly forfeit should release,
And with his Father work us a perpetual peace.

JOHN MILTON

Gifts

Christmas is a time of gift giving. Parents give presents to their children – husbands give to wives and wives to husbands – friends give to one another. There is a complete outpouring of giving at this time. A whole snow-storm of cards pours down on households all over the country. Why is this? How did it all start? The answer is in the first and greatest gift that has ever been made. God asked a woman to bestow this great gift upon mankind when he asked her to be the mother. For the gift lay in a manger in a cave at Bethlehem. That was the first Christmas and from that first Christmas all the others followed; from that first gift flowed a whole stream of gifts.

A gift is a way of saying 'I love you' to someone, so when God made his gift to men he was saying how much he loved them. He might have sent his Son direct to us in full manhood but that would have made his gift less precious and he wanted to give all that even he could give and so a little child was born of Mary. That little child born amid cold and poverty became the source of all the warmth and light and gaiety of Christmas. The love that inspires our gifts is but a faint reflection of the love that brought the greatest gift of all to come among us. God wrote his love story as all love stories are written in gifts. And the greatest chapter in that story was the giving of himself in human form.

Strength and Weakness

St Augustine said:

> He lies in a manger but contains the world; he sucks at the breasts, but feeds the angels; he is wrapped in swaddling clothes but vests us with immortality; he is suckled, but adored; he found no place at the inn, but makes for himself a temple in the hearts of believers. For in order that weakness might become strong, strength became weak.

The Chestnut

Eadmer, the Anglo-Saxon twelfth-century writer who was secretary to St Anselm, is credited with this analogy concerning the Immaculate Conception. Take the example from the chestnut. When it comes to birth in a tree of its kind, the husk shows rough and shaggy, bristling on every side with prickles. Inside, the nut itself takes shape (is conceived), and at first is like milky juice. There is no roughness, no unevenness; it has nothing prickly in itself, nor is it lacerated by anything around it. There gently and slowly it grows and swells and is nourished, until when it has been built up into its proper form and habit, bursting its husks in the hour of full maturity, it escapes from its prison, absolutely free from all puncture or roughness of prickles. Mark me, then, if God so guards the chestnut that in the very midst of thorns it is conceived and nourished and shaped without injury of thorns, could he not bestow upon the human body which he prepared for himself as a temple to abide in and out of which in the oneness of his person he was to assume that which would make him perfect man, could he not, I say, so preserve that same body that although it was conceived among the thorns of sin, it should itself be free from all puncture of thorns? Assuredly he could, if then he wished it, he also did it.

A Statute of Eton College

On every day of the year at a fitting hour of the evening all the choristers of our royal college together with the master in chant, shall enter the church at the sound of a bell, which shall be always rung except on Holy Thursday and Good Friday. And there, wearing surplices and ranged round a statue of the Blessed Virgin, with the candles lighted, shall sing solemnly and to the very best of their skill an antiphon of the Blessed Virgin, with the verse 'Ave Maria' and the prayer 'Meritis et precibus'.

The Black Virgin

In the hills above Barcelona lies Monserrat. It is halfway up a mountain and on it is the famous ancient church of Our Lady of Monserrat. Monserrat gets its name because the mountain is like the jagged teeth of a saw. Above the high altar of the church was built the statue of the Black Virgin; it is still there today. Close to the church is the great Benedictine Abbey.

Pilgrims from all over Europe used to flock to the shrine of the Black Virgin. On the Feast of the Annuciation in 1522 a pilgrim made his way up the mountain leading a mule. He limped a little from a past wound. He was dressed like a Spanish nobleman but when he arrived at the church of Our Lady he gave his fine clothes to a beggar in exchange for the beggar's mean attire. The pilgrim's name was Ignatius, a man who was to change much of the character of Europe. In the old world of the romances a newly-accoladed knight would prepare himself for his responsibilities by watching and praying from sunset to sunrise before the altar of Our Lady. Ignatius decided that he too would perform his 'vigil of arms' before the Black Virgin. To show that he had given up completely his former life as a soldier in the armies of Spain, Ignatius hung up his sword and dagger by Our Lady's side. He would become Our Lady's knight in the service of her Son. The next morning he left the Abbey, gave his mule to the prior and made his way on foot down the mountain.

The Wine of Gladness

When the wine of life is failing and our faith is weak, and our charity growing cold, we go to her that at Cana's feast interceded with her Divine Son for the replenishing of the wine of gladness; when our whole frame racks beneath the tempter we fly to the patronage of her Immaculate heart whose heel crushes the head of the serpent; when the cold hand of death is laid upon those whom we loved and our heart seems torn in twain because one with those who are gone then we climb the hill of Calvary to be consoled by the Mother of Sorrows who is also the source of our joy.

FULTON SHEEN

Joy

My soul magnifies the Lord and my spirit rejoices in God my Saviour. A soul magnifies the Lord which dedicates to the praise and service of God all its affections and proves its sense of the Divine Majesty by the observance of God's precepts. A spirit exults in God its Saviour which takes no thought of earthly pleasures, and is neither softened by prosperity nor crushed by adversity but which delights only in the remembrance of its creator for whom it looks for eternal salvation. But though these words are adapted to all the perfect, yet they could be uttered by none so fitly as by the Blessed Mother of God, who, by a special privilege, was both inflamed by a spiritual love of God and rejoiced in having conceived him in bodily form. Above all other saints she possessed the right to rejoice in her Jesus, that is her Saviour since she knew that he would derive his temporal birth from her. He was to be the Eternal Saviour of the world and who in one and the same person was her son and her Lord.

VENERABLE BEDE

Prayer by George Eliot

May I reach
That purest heaven, be to other souls
The cup of strength in some great agony,
Enkindle generous ardour, feel pure love,
Be the sweet presence of a good diffused,
And in diffusion ever more intense,
So shall I join the choir invisible
Whose music is the gladness of the world.

Much of the above could be applied to Our Lady though the author is not, of course, thinking of her.

The Queen

Whose is that throne, close to the throne of the God-Man Christ Jesus? Who is she, on whom those divine eyes, radiant with his Godhead, which survey all things in heaven and on earth, must rest with a special love, with the love of a son to his mother? What must be the love and humility of that highest being of the heavenly hierarchy, whether it be St Michael or any of the seraphim, belonging to those ranks which never fell, that he adores the condescension of God, not only in taking into himself our nature, but in placing nearest to himself the God-Man, his purely human mother, above every possible creature. For, grand and magnificent and highly-endowed as may be any of the highest creatures which God could create, none could have the nearness of her, the Mother of God.

EDWARD PUSEY

A Prayer for the Dying

Musetta in the opera *La Boheme* prays for the dying Mimi:

> Oh! Mary! Blessed Virgin
> Save, of thy mercy, this poor maiden.
> Save her, Madonna mine, from death.
> (A shade is put to the lamp)
> Here there should be a shade
> Because the lamp is flickering.
> And Oh! may she recover.
> Madonna, holy Mother, I merit not your pardon
> But our little Mimi is an angel from heaven.

The Changing Image

It is said of a certain miraculous image of Our Lady that its features change according to the person who stands in front of it. Sometimes there is a look of gracious attention, at others there is a stern rather unhappy look, at other times the features are sad, at others they are lit up with joy and human sympathy.

In every pious legend there is at least a grain of truth and this particular legend expresses the fact of Mary's interest in human affairs. She has a part to play in their activities. She knows that her Son died for them and she wants that death to be a vital element in their lives. What use would the title 'Our Mother' be if she were not interested in us? We know that we can get in touch with her by prayer but what use would prayer be if she had no care for us? She knows that her Son is still very active in our world. He is sacramentally present in it and continues to spread his kingdom through human agents. He still forgives through the sacraments; still shows his love in manifold ways. If he is so active then surely she is also. She, like him, has a human heart and she must feel sympathy and compassion for human suffering and human waywardness. Perhaps it should be us who look on Mary's face and ask ourselves whether we deserve a look of joy or one of sadness.

The Power and the Glory

Power can so easily corrupt but it will not do so if put at the service of love. Mary knew that alone she was powerless. Her love for God gave her power because it brought a response of power from God. So it was that one who was only a village girl living in a despised village became a queen who ruled over all peoples from her throne close to that of her son. God did great things for her giving her power for a time over himself when born at Bethlehem. The infant God lay in his weakness in a manger. She had the task of feeding him and caring for him. The child who was to say when he had grown up that all power is given to me in heaven and on earth, could not even speak. She not only gave to us our redeemer when he was born but she protected him from harm until he was capable of looking after himself. No wonder then that all generations would call her blessed. She who did not seek any glory became the glory of mankind – our tainted nature's solitary boast. But it was not a glory easily gained. A Roman philosopher said, 'It is a rough road that leads to the heights of greatness.' Certainly Mary had a rough road to traverse but her courage in walking it only added to her greatness. We can surely apply to her what the poet wrote:

O what a glory doth this world put on,
For him who with fervent heart goes forth,
Under the bright and glorious sky and looks
On duties well performed and days well spent.

LONGFELLOW

God's Will

Both the first and the last words of Christ in the Gospels refer to his relationship with his Father. He was always about his Father's business. He always did the things that pleased the Father. He said: 'My meat is to do the will of him who sent me.' He was obedient to his Father even to the death on a cross. His dying words were, 'Father, into thy hands I commend my spirit.' The will of God came first in his life. He followed it though it hurt his mother, as when he remained in the temple without her knowing it.

St Mark's Gospel tells us that Christ entered a house: 'And his mother and his brethren came, and standing outside they sent to him. And a crowd was sitting about him and they said to him, "Your mother and your brethren are outside asking for you." And he replied: "Who are my mother and my brethren?" And looking round on those who sat with him he said: "Here are my mother and my brethren. Whoever does the will of God is my brother and sister and mother."'

His words were no rebuke to his mother. Christ is simply making a comparison between those who are related to him by blood and the very many who can claim spiritual relationship with him because, like him, they do the will of God. On another occasion, also recorded in St Luke, a woman cries out: 'Blessed is the womb that bore you', to which Christ replies: 'Rather blessed are they who hear the word of God and keep it.' Both these occasions are exalting the kingdom above the natural claims of flesh and blood and Mary had to progress in her pilgrimage of faith.

The Kingdom

The Magi story is one of mystery and mysticism symbolic of that striving after truth that has been the mainspring of so much human endeavour. It is the function of wisdom to seek the truth and these wise men were endowed, not only with human learning, but also with that supernatural insight that enabled them to see the truth hidden away in a poor cottage in a distant land.

They came in search of a king. 'Where is he who has been born King of the Jews?', they asked. No doubt they did not fully understand what kind of king they were looking for, but they came to their journey's end: 'And going in the house they saw the child with Mary his mother.' Their actions showed that they realised that here was more than an earthly monarch. They gave precious gifts and bowed down in worship.

What did they really comprehend about Jesus? What did they think of Mary who had all the appearance of a poor village girl amid surroundings of great poverty? What did Mary herself think? We cannot enter their minds, but at least we know something about Mary's from the words spoken to her by the angel:

He will be great and will be called
the Son of the Most High;
and the Lord will give him
the throne of his father David,
and he will reign over the house of Jacob for ever;
and of his kingdom there will be no end.

Mary must often have pondered those words. She knew that in some way her son was to be a king and to found a kingdom. How he was to do it she did not know.

Candlemas

Forty days after the birth of Jesus, Mary and Joseph took the child to the temple to offer him up to God in accordance with the law. This entrance of Christ into his Father's house is symbolised by the procession of candles. Christ is the Light of the World; the lighted candles represent this and the light reflected on the face of their carriers shows that they are Christians, followers of Christ.

There is a real sense in which it can be said that those lighted candles were lit by Mary. After all she gave the Light to the world. She was the generator of light – a light which was to dispel the darkness of sin which had covered the world. John the Baptist had said that he was not the light but had come to give testimony of the light. Mary too could have said those words. Though she gave the light she was not the light. Simeon made this clear when he spoke of Christ as the light to enlighten the Gentiles and the glory of his people Israel. Mary's glory was the reflection of that glory. Christ was to say to us later, 'So let your light shine before men that they may see your good works.' This light within us comes from the source of all light, Christ, the Light of the World.

Candlemas 1605

Today the two Jesuits, Garnet and Oldcorne, were brought to London and were lodged at the Gatehouse. They have been very kindly used since their taking. Garnet being lodged in the house of Sir Henry and his family. On Candlemas Day there was a great dinner made to end Christmas and all drank the health of the king bare-headed. There came in, accompanying the wine, a white wax candle lighted with Jesus on one side and Maria on the other. So Garnet, desiring to see the candle, took it in his hands and gave it to Oldcorne saying that he was glad that he had carried a holy candle on Candlemas Day.

Criminal Trials

What Candles Teach Us

First, that God is a consuming fire, whereof the very burning candle doth warn us. Secondly, that as the candle being one kind of creature consisteth of fire, wax and wick; so Christ consisteth of the Godhead, soul, and flesh, all being in one person. Therefore on Candlemas Day by carrying a holy candle we do well represent Our Lady carrying Christ to the temple in her arms. Thirdly, we ought always to have the fire of charity in our hearts as the wise virgins had. Last of all, by the torches which are lighted at the singing of the gospel, it is signified, that the word of God is the light of the soul.

LAWRENCE VAUX

Suppression

When he was Archbishop of Canterbury in 1571, Archbishop Grindal published an injunction to the laity:

No person or persons whatsover shall wear beads, or pray, either in Latin or in English, upon beads, or knots, or any other like superstitious thing; nor shall pray upon any popish Latin or English primer, or other like book, nor shall burn any candles in the church superstitiously upon the feast of the Purification of the Virgin Mary, commonly called Candlemas Day; nor shall resort to any popish priest for shrift or auricular confession in Lent or at any other time; nor shall worship any cross or any image or picture upon the same, nor give any reverence thereunto, nor superstitiously shall make upon themselves the sign of the cross when they first enter into a church to pray, nor shall say De Profundis for the dead, or rest at any cross in carrying any corpse to burying, nor shall leave any little crosses of wood there.

Mary and the Mass

The Mass is the same sacrifice as that of Calvary because it is offered by the same priest, Christ himself. It has the same victim and it is offered for the same purpose – the glory of God and the sanctification of mankind.

There are two scenes in Mary's life that not only remind one of the Mass but also show her intimate connection with it. In the first scene she took the infant Christ to the temple at Jerusalem and presented him to the Father, making an offering of her son to him. This was not simply the offering of a child. It included all that that child would become; even his death upon a cross formed part of the offering. This was emphasised by the words of Simeon that the child would be a sign contradiction and that a sword would pierce his mother's heart.

This leads to the second scene which took place on Calvary with Mary close to the cross. Most mothers would have resented what was happening there but not Mary. She joined with her son in a free offering of himself to the Father. In every Mass people make an offering of Christ to his Father but Mary's part in this offering was far more intimate than any other. Christ was the sole mediator between God and man but Mary gave the mediator to the world and her suffering formed part of his redemptive work. His was the passion; hers the compassion. He was the redeemer of the world; she was the mother of the redeemer. It is good then for us to turn our minds sometimes at Mass to Mary and join with her in our offering of Christ to the Father. With her we stand at the foot of the cross since every Mass is that of Calvary.

A Beautiful Legend

In the *Apocrypha* we learn that it came to pass that the blessed Mary was wearied by the too great heat of the sun in the desert; and seeing a palm tree she said to Joseph: 'Let me rest a little under the shadow of this tree.' Joseph therefore led her to the tree and caused her to sit. And when the blessed Mary had sat down there, she looked at the palm and saw that it was full of fruit. So she said to Joseph, 'I desire that I may be able to partake of the fruit of this tree!' And Joseph said to her, 'I wonder that you say this when you see what a height the palm is.' Then the little child Jesus, sitting with a glad countenance in his mother's lap said to the palm, 'O tree, bend down thy branches, and with thy fruit refresh my mother.' And straightway at his word the palm bowed down its top to the feet of the blessed Mary, and they gathered from it fruit with which to be refreshed. Now after they had gathered all its fruit, it remained bowed down, waiting to rise at his command. Then Jesus said:

> Raise thee, O palm, and be strong and be a partner with my trees which are in the Paradise of my father. And open from thy roots a spring of water which is hidden in the earth; and let waters flow from it to our satisfying.

And immediately it rose, and there began to flow forth at its root a most pure fount of waters, very cool and exceedingly clear. Now when they saw the fount of water they rejoiced with great joy; and they, and all the beasts and cattle were satisfied; wherefore they gave thanks to God.

Perfection

Mary is the highest example of human perfection and of created happiness. And this great fact strikes down a thousand theories. In every earthly sense of the word she is weak, as she is lowly, poor and humble; and yet she is perfect as no one else ever was perfect. And her perfection is the work of a sublime grace, which puts her nature in order and sets her higher powers free in God. The Immaculate Conception is the mystery of God's strength in weakness, of his height in humility, of his glory in purity. And when we contemplate that glorious creature, in whom from the first instant of her creation the image of God was so beautiful, in whom grace found no resistance, whose aspirations grew ever more divine; when we contemplate that living shrine of the Holy Spirit's fire; when we look up to that animated brightness, as clothed with the sun and crowned with the stars, and seated next her Son abode Cherub and Seraph; and when we hear her truthful lips proclaim, 'The Lord has looked down upon the humility of his handmaid ... He has lifted up the lowly', our pride sinks down rebuked, our false ambition stands reproved, our sensuous strength betrays the weakness of its origin, and our confidence in the perfection of our nature is discovered to be that broken reed of which we had so often heard in vain. The condition of perfection is shown to be chaste humility, and the source of perfection the grace of Christ. And that grace must come to us as Christ prescribes, and not as we choose.

BISHOP ULLATHORNE

Mother's Day

An ex-president of Texas University, gave this address for Mother's Day, 1915:

Mother, for whom words never have been, never can be coined, with which to weave the wreath of glory that we would place upon thy brow – mother, by whom God became man, by whom the human race has thus been linked for ever to the throne of God-mother, the light of whose eyes was the first light that shone upon the babe of Bethlehem – mother, whose face was the first face into which the infant Jesus looked – mother, who alone of all God's servants, angels, archangels, seraphim and cherubim cradled Deity in thine arms and laid him on thy bosom and held him to thy breast – mother, who taught the feet of the infant Son of God to walk – mother, the first word that the lips of the babe that was God and man learned to lisp – mother, who guided the footsteps of the Son of God and Son of Man through a spotless youth to a spotless manhood – mother, who followed the Son of God, Son of thy bone and flesh of thy flesh, to the cross to ignominious death – mother, through whom Heaven itself was for ever changed when the Son of Mary, as he hung upon the cross died and took his place for ever upon the throne of God – mother, to this sin-darkened world you gave the infant Jesus, God and man, to whom you gave to Heaven the Lamb of God who is the light of Heaven – mother, standing not beneath the cross but beneath the glory of the throne of God and of the Lamb, that throne now resplendent with the glory with which thy Son has enshrouded it, one and all we rise up and call thee blessed and place upon thy brow our richest diadem. We crown thee queen of our hearts. We give thee first place in all of God's creation.

Wine

The little village of Cana in Galilee has become famous because the Son of God and his mother graced it with their presence. It was there that Christ performed his first miracle. He changed something very ordinary into something precious and richer. St John calls his miracles signs and it is the sign that is important here. It is surely not fanciful to say that Christ and his mother were bringing out the sacredness of marriage by their taking part in the festival. Both Mary and her son wanted it to be a happy occasion and when the wine ran out she pointed it out to her son who in turn provided the remedy.

We should then not fix our attention simply on the miracle. We should try to see signs and lessons even though all of them may not have been intended by St John. The marriage, like the wine, must not fail. With Our Lady's intercession and Christ's help it will not fail. We can also meditate on the fact that if Christ could turn water into wine surely he could turn wine into his own blood. Or we can see Christ as the vine, the giver of wine.

The one who was to offer his blood wine for the salvation of the human race offers it every day all over the world today. Or we can see, in Mary's words, 'They have no wine' the cry of many people. They are without the rich graces which her son can give through the shedding of his blood. If they pray to her there is great hope that these graces will come full to overflowing. Did Christ himself see in the wine an image of his own blood which would one day be poured out on a cross? We can at least know this his 'hour' had not yet come. That 'hour' was his passion and it was to be his mother's compassion.

Inspiration

John Ruskin wrote:

> After the most careful examination, neither as adversary nor
> friend, of the influence of Catholicity for good or evil, I am
> persuaded that the worship of the Madonna has been one of
> the noblest and most vital graces, and has never been
> otherwise than productive of true holiness of life and purity
> of character. There has probably not been an innocent
> cottage home throughout the length and breadth of Europe
> during the whole period of vital Christianity, in which the
> imagined presence of the Madonna has not given sanctity to
> the humblest duties and comfort to the sorest trials of the
> lives of women; and every brightest and loftiest achievement
> of the arts and strength of manhood has been the fulfillment
> of the prophecy of the Israelite maiden. 'He that is mighty
> hath magnified me and holy is his name.'

Can one doubt that our modern world needs Our Lady to bring
a message of hope and spiritual beauty to those who toil amid
drab, ugly and oppressive surroundings, to bring warmth to
what is cold, dehumanising, mechanical, to bring light where
there is darkness and gloom of mind, to show courage to those
who are afraid and peace to those without it? For holiness
creates a sense of reality in synthetic culture; it is an antidote to
cheap sensationalism, an earnestness amid trivialities. The vision
of Mary then opens out new vistas and pathways amid the dark
jungle of uncertainties and doubts which cloud human minds.
She points the way to a more profound and better life, showing
how it must have its roots in an inner world governed by the
Spirit of God. Economic planning, political endeavour, pacts
and alliances cannot in themselves bring a peaceful and happy
world. Mary and her son must become involved in its affairs, for
without them there will be no true peace and joy.

Prayer

We ask Our Lady to pray for us now and at the hour of our death. Some people may say that praying to Our Lady is pointless. Why not pray straight to Christ? Did not Christ say, 'No one goes to the Father except through me'? How then can we go to him through Mary? Many Christians give the obvious answer that Mary is the mother of Jesus and therefore must have great influence with him. A mother's love can be very powerful. This way of thinking has great validity. But it is not the whole answer. We pray to Christ because he is our Saviour. He died on the cross for us all. Each of us receives the power of the cross provided we open out our hearts to receive it; this we do by our prayers. But Mary had an intimate part to play in our salvation. Not only did she give us the Saviour but she stood beneath the cross in prayer. It is surely natural for us to join our prayers with hers.

Christ spoke to his mother from the cross. He had all that she was suffering in mind. She was a part of himself; in love and understanding they were one. So in praying to her we are praying to him. The two of them are inseparable, not in power, but in unity of purpose, and though we may think of her as on her own, she never is. She is nothing without him. Our prayers go then through Mary to Christ. And what is of the utmost importance to realise is the part she plays in the life of the Church. The Second Vatican Council stated that she is intimately united with the Church and added: 'Hence the Church in her apostolic work also rightly looks to her who brought forth Christ, conceived by the Holy Spirit and born of the Virgin, so that through the Church Christ may be born and grow in the hearts of the faithful also.'

The Challenge of Our Time

There was once a series of talks entitled 'The Challenge of our Time' on the radio. All the speakers, whether they were historians, scientists or philosophers, were agreed on one point, that there was something radically wrong with our present day civilisation. Each had a different remedy. One found it in bettering economic conditions, another appealed to the shade of Karl Marx. Others did mention Christianity but only in a superficial way.

The challenge of our time is the challenge of faith. Men need something to live for and to live by. They need a common cause and a common loyalty. And if one were to ask what element of faith needs most to be restored and loved, the answer surely would be found in a woman who became the mother of God who came down to earth to show the way to live and die. Men need to return to the spirit which inspired architects to raise beautiful buildings in honour of the child and his mother; which inspired the chisel of the sculptor and guided the hand of the painter or led men on to incredible deeds in the service of their fellow men. It was a time when Columbus named his ship the *Santa Maria*, Fra Angelico would kneel to paint his Madonnas, when Moslems were beating upon the gates of Europe and people went down on their knees with their rosaries in their hands and prayed their way to survival.

One of the popes said that Europe had killed its past. It is the task of all of us, in so far as we are able, to show to others who know little of Mary and her child, what spiritual happiness and worth there is in love and reverence for them.

Vatican II and Our Lady

In the Second Vatican Council (Vatican II) the final chapter in the Constitution on the Church was devoted to Our Lady. A separate document about her was contemplated but the Council fathers, after much discussion, decided that she should not be treated in isolation. They preferred to link her role more closely with that of the Church. And they were surely right. Mary must be seen as playing a vital part in the work of the Church. After all, she was intimately connected with it since the Church is the mystical body of Christ. She is thus the mother of the Church as the Council indicated. 'Taught by the Holy Spirit, the Catholic Church honours her with filial affection and piety as a most devoted mother.'

The Council also wanted to emphasise Mary's part in the work of salvation. It states: 'The union of the mother with her son in the work of salvation was manifested from the time of Christ's virginal conception up to his death.' It also urges theologians and preachers of the divine word that in treating of the unique dignity of the mother of God they carefully and equally avoid the falsity of exaggeration on the one hand and the excess of narrow-mindedness on the other. The answer is to see Mary as she appears in Scripture.

The Council ends the document with the prayer: 'That she who aided the beginnings of the Church by her prayers, may now, exalted as she is above all the angels and saints, intercede with her son in the fellowship of all the saints.' Her intercession is implored for all peoples, Christians and non-Christians, so that they become united into one people of God.

Mirror of Justice

A mirror reflects a likeness. The reflection depends for its existence completely upon the reality. It has no substance of itself. If the object departs so does the image in the mirror.

Mary is the mirror of justice. All her great qualities are reflections from those of her son. She does not exist as the woman we know without him. She is beautiful in soul, immaculate, full of grace because of him. She moves and acts at his command because her will is united with his. We cannot then separate Mary from Christ without destroying the whole meaning of her personality. It was for him that she was created. God prepared this 'house of gold' by sending his Holy Spirit who is the living source of all supernatural perfection.

Mary, it has been said, is a dream of God expressed for man's delight. For man, to know such loveliness in human form is to know what purity and innocence is. For in spite of all the sins and evil in human beings there is deep down, even if not always recognised, a longing for a golden age of innocence and intimacy with God that was lost in the garden at the beginning of the world.

When Mary stood at the foot of the cross she reflected in herself her son's sufferings and he, in his turn, experienced in himself this added pain of seeing her sorrow and anguish. But since her life was one of union with his, her suffering and sorrow became part of his Passion's redemption even though she was in no way the redeemer. What is true is that she united herself with his work of redemption more closely than any other human being.

The Sword

Hilaire Belloc wrote:

> Our Lady stood beside the cross
> A little space apart
> And when she heard Our Lord cry out
> A sword went through her heart

Some thirty years before, Mary and Joseph had taken their child to the temple to present him to his Father. Simeon had taken the child in his arms, fulfilling his lifelong desire to see the hope of Israel. In prophetic vision he had seen in the child 'a sign of contradiction', one who held the key to the mystery of life, upon whose acceptance or rejection man's salvation or ruin depended. Also he saw that a sword would pierce his mother's heart. Love, pain, sorrow, joy, light and darkness – these were the contradictions in which the salvation of men would be worked out or their fate sealed. Joy and sorrow were never far apart in the lives of Christ and his mother as in all human lives. On Calvary the sorrow reached its peak in Mary. This was inevitable. What mother would not have felt intense sorrow in such circumstances? Yet with it there must have been a deep interior peace. That little child whom she had offered up in the temple long ago was now making an offering of himself to the Father and she was joining with him in the offering. He went to his death willingly, obedient to his Father's will. She made a willing oblation to that same Father in spite of the agony it entailed.

Christ's heart was pierced by a lance and blood and water flowed out. This showed that he had given everything. The sword that pierced Mary's heart was that lance's counterpart. It was a sign that she had given all.

Mary and John

When picturing the scene of Christ on the cross with his mother beneath it, we naturally think of the sorrow of Mary for her son's suffering. We must not forget that Christ, for his part, knew what his mother was going through. He knew the dreadful pain his wounds were causing her. His cry from the cross committing her to John was a cry from his heart to comfort and console her. John was one of his close friends and he knew that she would find help and solace in his home.

But there is more to the incident than that. Always with John's writing we must look for the spiritual symbols embodied in his words. Commentators have seen in this incident the bringing into being of the new family of God born from the cross. Without the cross there is no Church. And since Mary gave the Redeemer to the world she gave, in a sense, the cross also. She thus became a figure of power in the Church, having a vital part to play with her son. It is wrong to call her co-redemptrix. She did not redeem mankind. Only her son did that. In fact she needed redemption herself. What she did do was to cooperate more closely than anybody else in her son's work of redemption, just as it is our duty as Christians as far as we are able, to further his redemptive work. The world will continue to need redemption until its end and Christ who, once and for all, offered the means of salvation through his death on the cross, now expects his followers to carry on his work through prayer and good works.

Goethe's Death

Fainter and fainter grew his breath;
His hour had come – the hour of death.
'Oh see,' the dying poet said,
'The woman with the lovely head.'
Sweet Virgin Mother, ever dear,
Oh, tell me, didst thou linger near?

Death's shadows close and closer crept;
And ere his last the poet slept
He faintly uttered, 'Light, more light';
Then silence fell and all was night.
Had light come down and kissed him there?
Or were his dying words a prayer?

ANON

Beneath the Cross

It was an immortal scene. The mother motionless, like a piece of sculpture carved out of the darkness. Above her the great black arms of the cross with the shackled figure nailed to it. All nature seemed to be mourning for its maker and the mother, lost in the gloom, must have felt the terrible wrench of separation from the one she loved. Who can express the bleak stillness and the inner tide of sorrow sweeping through the mother's mind and heart as the flame of life in her son diminished and gradually flickered into extinction? St Bernard says somewhere that in the case of the other martyrs love decreased their pain, but with Mary, the more she loved the more she suffered. Love added fire to her sufferings.

Christ did not come into the world to banish pain, not even

that of his mother. He did come to give strength to bear it. He also gave a meaning to it, to those who endure it with faith and love. Love of God and suffering are so often bound together in this life. They certainly were in the case of Christ and his mother. This is not because God is cruel and takes delight in suffering but because love is a purifying force and thus the enemy of evil. Christ had taken upon himself the burden of all humanity's sin and through his supreme act of love had conquered it. Love then was the ultimate reason for the agony of Calvary. It was a love that gave all up to the pain of separation. His cry of desolation was a proof of this and it was a cry that found its echo in his mother's heart.

Mary Speaks

When he was small I washed and fed him; dressed him in his little garments and combed the rings of his hair. When he cried I comforted him; when he was hurt I kissed away the pain; and when darkness fell I sang him to sleep. Now he goes faint and fasting in the dust, and his hair is tangled with thorns. They will strip him naked to the sun and hammer the nails into his living flesh, and the great darkness will cover him. And there is nothing I can do, nothing at all.

DOROTHY SAYERS

Battle Against Evil

St John, in the Book of Revelation, gives a picture of a woman clothed with the sun and confronted by a dragon who 'stood before the woman who was about to bear a child, that he might devour the child when she brought it forth. She gave birth to a son, a male child who is to rule the nations with a rod of iron, and her child was caught up by God and to his throne.' Much discussion has centred upon the significance of the woman. The common opinion is that she stands in some way as a sign of the Church. At the same time it is clear that it is also an allusion to the mother of Jesus. She is the one about whom it was prophesied that her son would crush the serpent's head.

The world is a battlefield for the forces of good and evil. Mary's son is the protagonist of all who fight evil. He is the conqueror of evil. Round the cross the forces of evil raged as Christ said they would. 'The prince of this world comes and he has no power over me', he said. Mary was at the centre of the battlefield. The dragon was endeavouring to destroy her son's work. It was because of evil that her son was on the cross. At the same time it was through the cross that Christ would 'rule the nations'. He would complete the victory when he was caught up to God and his throne by his resurrection. Mother and son are together the enemies of evil. We pray to her 'Refuge of sinners' to obtain pardon for the times when we have been tainted by sin, knowing that it is a thing unheard of that anyone who has recourse to her protection will go unaided.

Standing by the Cross

There stood by the cross of Jesus his most holy and ever-virgin Mother Mary.

And how could'st thou stand? Whence came thy strength? Of a certainty, thy body was not of steel or stone, that this day thou couldst be pierced so many times by the sword of sorrow, and crucified so many times and wounded together with thy son, nevertheless thou didst stand there firm both in body and soul. Perhaps it was that those strong and rough nails held thee also fast upon the cross of thy son, so that thou couldst not fall. But far more strongly did thy mighty love, love stronger than death, bear thee up, so that thou couldst not fall. Thou stoodest, therefore, the immovable column of the faith.

Therefore thou stoodest by his cross, and didst adore his Godhead in spirit. Truly thou stoodest like some strong tower in which the king who had set forth on a long journey had hidden the precious treasure of faith. And because all grief and compassion that spring from love are great according to the measure of love, therefore, because thy love was beyond all measure, thy grief was utterly measureless.

JOHN TAULER

A Prayer

O my Lord and Saviour, support me in my last hour by the strong arms of thy sacraments and the fragrance of thy consolations. Let thy absolving word be said over me, and the holy oil sign and seal me, and let thy own body be my food, and thy blood my sprinkling; and let thy Mother Mary come to me, and my angel whisper peace to me, and thy glorious saints and my own dear patrons smile on me, that in and through them all I may die, as I desire to live, in thy Church, in thy faith and in thy love.

CARDINAL NEWMAN

Death

What were the thoughts of Our Lady as she held the dead body of her son in her arms? She had pondered over him so often in the past but that was when he was alive. She was looking at a body covered with blood and wounds. She could see the stripes made by the scourging and the whole disfigurement of his frame. Did she know of the great transformation that would take place in three days time? We do not know if Christ told his mother about it. It is far more likely that he wanted her to be the mother of faith until the resurrection. Always he had been a mystery to her so it would be till the end of his life. She might not have understood the full meaning of what was happening but her attitude was certainly 'Be it done unto me according to thy word.' She might not have known what was to happen to her son but her faith remained strong and firm. Certainly her sorrow did not diminish. Her son had died amid darkness and darkness had entered her being. The death of such a wonderful son under such terrible circumstances was enough to reduce herself near to death. She had heard his words spoken from the cross and the words 'It is finished' must have come especially home to her. She knew it meant that his mission had been accomplished. She knew of his work for others when he was alive – how he went about doing good and healing so many bodies and souls. Now he had met a criminal's death. The sword of sorrow had indeed pierced Mary's heart but one can be sure that mingling with her sorrow and allied to her faith there was a gleam of hope that somehow all would in the end be well.

Loneliness

Love was the ultimate reason for all the agony of Calvary. It was a love that gave all even to the pain of separation. Christ's cry of desolation was a proof of this and it was a cry that found its echo in his mother's heart. A screen of darkness fell between her and her son emphasising the gap that lay between them. His loneliness and distress belonged to her also. Siegfried Sassoon in his poem 'Alone' wrote:

> I thought of age, and loneliness and change.
> I thought how strange we grow when we're alone.
> And how unlike selves that meet and talk,
> And blow the candles out, and say good night,
> Alone . . . the word is life endured and known,
> It is the stillness where our spirits walk
> And all but inmost faith is overthrown.

Mary's faith was put to a great test on Calvary but in spite of all the darkness and suffering it always held firm. Her loneliness did not separate her from the God who had done such great things for her. She was there when the light of her son's life was extinguished and she heard him say his good night as he commended his soul to his Father. It was a dark end to his life but certainly no end to her faith in him. This was the greatest moment of loneliness. She was separated from her son by his death and it was also the greatest moment for faith. She knew he had gone willingly to death so she joined her will with his.

Pieta

In St Peter's, Rome, may be seen Michelangelo's marble group representing the blessed virgin with the body of the dead Saviour on her knees. The critics of the time objected to the youthful appearance of the mother but he defended it on the ground that it afforded an additional proof of her pure and spotless character. 'You forget', he said to one stubborn critic 'that Our Lady was an immaculate virgin; sin never had dominion over her, the beauty of her youth could never fade.' He has inscribed his name on the girdle of the virgin. It is said to be the only work on which he did it.

Even in her deepest moments of sorrow Mary remains in our minds as perennially youthful. It is a young mother who holds the dead Christ. It is an attractive picture in spite of mutilation and disfigurement. The son in her arms is covered with blood and wounds. His countenance is ravaged and unsightly. The beauty of the scene comes, not from its outward display, but from its inner significance. Here is an overwhelming love; and though it appears on the surface to be a scene of complete failure, we know that it is very near to glory and victory.

Mark Anthony looked down on the dead body of Caesar and said:

O mighty Caesar, dost thou lie so low?
Are all they conquests, glories, triumphs, spoils
Shrunk to this little measure?

Our Lady could not speak that way of her son. His conquests, glories, triumphs, spoils have not shrunk to nothing. His very death is their gain. Mary must have known in the depths of her sorrow that all was not lost.

The Joy of the Resurrection

Scripture gives no account of Christ's appearance to his mother after his resurrection but surely we can take it for granted that he did appear to her. Here is one instance where silence had no need to be broken. She who shared in his sufferings should certainly share his joy. She who had held his bleeding wounded body in her arms in death would undoubtedly see him alive with his wounds now symbols of victory and love.

Christ transforms human nature. Through death he gives new life. Where there is trouble and anxiety he brings peace; and where there is sorrow joy. His risen presence must have meant an immense transformation in Mary's life. One can imagine the immense tide of joy that would sweep through the heart of a mother whose son had been reported dead, perhaps in war, and who then suddenly came back to her alive and well. For Mary it was coming back from death itself of the most wonderful of all sons. The very pain she endured emphasised the happiness. It was a joy born out of suffering.

Mary could not have lost hope in her son. Though there was much she had not understood her hope remained firm and had its reward. St Clement of Alexandria wrote: 'If you do not hope you will not find what is beyond your hope.' Mary found what was beyond her hope when she clasped the living Christ in her arms. His resurrection was her resurrection also. The story that had begun at Nazareth had come to its climax. To many it had ended with the cross but for her it was an ending of glory. She could echo John's words: 'We have seen his glory, glory as of the only Son from the Father' and she could add 'my son also'.

Raised from the Grave

One reason for believing in Our Lady's Assumption is that her divine Son loved her too much to let her body remain in the grave. A second reason is this, that she was not only dear to our Lord as a mother is dear to her son, but also that she was so transcendently holy, so full, so overflowing with grace. Adam and Eve were created upright and sinless, and had a large measure of God's grace bestowed upon them; and, in consequence, their bodies would never have crumbled into dust, had they not sinned; upon which it was said to them 'Dust thou art and unto dust thou shalt return.' If Eve, the beautiful daughter of God, never would have become dust and ashes unless she had sinned, shall we not say that Mary, having never sinned, retained the gift which Eve by sinning lost? What had Mary done to forfeit the privilege given to our first parents in the beginning? Was her comeliness to be turned into corruption, and her fine gold to become dim, with reason assigned? Impossible. Therefore we believe that, though she died for a short hour, as did Our Lord himself, yet, like him, and by his almighty power, she was raised again from the grave.

CARDINAL NEWMAN

Madonna

In his anthology, *The Madonna of the Cherries*, Field Marshall Lord Wavell included these beautiful words:

> Your red-gold hair, your slowly smiling face
> Your pride in your dear son, your King of Kings,
> Fruits of the kindly earth, and truth and grace,
> Colour and light, and all warm lovely things –
> For all that loveliness, that warmth, that light,
> Blessed Madonna I go back to fight.

Queen of Heaven

The picture of a vast number of people 'whom no man can number' singing together before a great throne where God sits in majesty and close by, other thrones on which Christ and his mother reign with majestic countenances is, of course, a figment of the imagination. It is legitimate, as John did in the Book of Revelations, to picture Paradise in such a way but obviously he meant his description to be symbolic. The term 'Queen of Heaven' is itself symbolic. What then does it mean? We can, as Christian devotion states, say that it means that Our Lady is greater in dignity than all the saints and angels. But though we may pray to her in those terms we may find it difficult to meditate on it. The answer is not to think of her in isolation but close to her son. The whole of her wonderful and strange story stems from him. It has affinities with the Cinderella story.

The human race in sin is the prototype of the ugly sisters, but God has taken her and clothed her with immaculate grace giving her a share of his glory and eventually taking her to the splendour of Paradise. John, in the Book of Revelation, writes: 'A great sign appeared in Heaven, a woman clothed with the sun and the moon under her feet, and on her head a crown of twelve stars'. Those words apply to the Church but also to Mary who is a sign of the Church. There she is amid the communion of saints interceding for us and winning graces from her son. So many graces and blessings have been won from her. She does not, of course, give them herself. She intercedes with her Son who cannot deny her what she asks for. After all she is his mother and our mother also.

Pentecost

Christianity was born in its fullness on the day of Pentecost. Thereafter the indwelling presence of the Holy Spirit would always be felt in the heart of Christendom. We are told in the Acts of the Apostles that Mary, the mother of Jesus was in the upper room with the apostles. In that room was gathered the first members of the Church. There was the tiny seed of which Christ spoke which he prophesied would develop into a mighty tree. There was the tiny piece of yeast which was to leaven the whole mass of the world. From that room the Church of Christ would start its work and continue to grow in numbers and holiness through the ages.

The presence of Mary shows that she had her part to play in this growth. She was to be at the heart of the Church. What did the Holy Spirit do for her at that time? Surely he was to reveal to her secrets about her son which she had not realised before. In the past she had pondered over many things about him and there were things she had not understood. She had always been the woman of faith but now, as the apostles' minds were enlightened about the full implications of Christ's teaching, so, but in a more profound way, was hers. She shared in Pentecost with her own endowment of grace. She had know Jesus far better than the apostles had known him. She shared their experience as the tongues of flame from Heaven hovered over them, but for her the awakening to a perfect knowledge of Christ was on a higher level because of her fullness of grace. Also because she was Christ's mother she was more able to approach near to his wonderful personality both human and divine.

The Assumption

The Assumption of Mary is the fruit of her Immaculate Conception and of her loving service of God. It springs from them quite naturally. The fact is not mentioned in Scripture but the indications of it are there. She was after all the well-favoured one in whom the glory of God's grace shone in its fullness. She was therefore completely without the corrupting influence of sin. She was the ideal of purity and loveliness of being. Her body was never used as an agent of evil; her eyes and lips and hands and feet were used solely in the service of God. Just as her son could say 'I do always the things that please the Father', she could say 'Be it done unto me according to thy will.' Her will was always united with that of her son in giving praise, love and service to God. Mary's body had been the chosen dwelling place of God's own son. It was therefore a sanctified body.

Since she was incorruptible in life both in body and soul surely she should be the same at the end of her life on earth. And so it happened. She was taken body and soul to the Christ who was waiting for her. Her incorrupt body became the outward sign of her purity of soul. We would do well to meditate on St Paul's words concerning the resurrection of the body and ask ourselves how much of them applies or does not apply to Mary. 'What is sown corruptible, rises incorruptible; what is sown dishonoured rises in glory; what is sown in weakness is raised in power; what is sown a natural body rises a spiritual body'. However we apply some of those words to Our Lady, one thing we cannot say about her, that she was 'sown dishonoured'.

Womanhood

What special characteristics of Mary made their impact on the culture of our civilisation? Certainly her purity and her privilege of being the mother of God. These had an enormous influence on art. The art galleries of the world would be very much poorer if she had never lived. Music too would have lost much without her and, of course, sculpture. She enkindled the imagination of people with a vision of another world. For some sixteen centuries the artists of Europe have concerned themselves with the portrayal of the Madonna. Satisfying presentations of the Madonna are at least as numerous in sculpture as they are in painting. She is presented in a vast variety of ways both in legends but chiefly because of what Scripture says of her. One great example of her influence is seen as the Madonna of Mercy who extends her cloak to shelter the poor and suffering and most particularly in death. As the mother sorrowing at the foot of the cross, or holding the dead body of her son she has become the symbol of consolation for human grief just as her motherhood has become the symbol of maternal love. And it would be hard to decide which of these two symbols has the more profoundly affected not only the arts but human devotion.

The Ideal

The world is governed by its ideals and seldom or never has there been one which exercised a more profound or, upon the whole, a more salutary influence than the medieval conception of the Virgin. For the first time woman was elevated to her rightful position, and the sanctity of weakness was recognised as well as the sanctity of sorrow. No longer the slave or the toy of man no longer associated only with ideas of degradation and of sensuality, woman rose, in the person of the Virgin Mother, into a new sphere and became the object of a reverential homage of which antiquity had no conception. Love was idealised. The moral charm and beauty of female excellence was fully felt. Into a harsh and ignorant and benighted age this ideal type infused a conception of gentleness and purity unknown to the proudest civilisation of the past.

W. E. H. LECKY